A HOUSE THAT CONTENDS

Lou Engle & Sam Cerny

Copyright © 2010, 2019 by Lou Engle and Sam Cerny

All scripture quotations, unless otherwise indicated, are taken from the New King James Version®. Copyright© 1982 by Thomas Nelson, Inc. Used by permission. All rights reserved.

The moral right of the authors has been asserted.
All rights reserved. No part of this publication may be reproduced, stored in a retrieval system, or transmitted, in any form or by any means, without the prior permission in writing of the publisher, nor be otherwise circulated in any form of binding or cover other than that in which it is published and without a similar condition including this condition being imposed on the subsequent publisher.

ISBN 978-1-6956-3789-4

Lou Engle Ministries
102 S Tejon St. STE 1100
Colorado Springs, CO 80903

*There are giants in the land.
These giants are meant to fall.*

CONTENTS

1. Giants Are Meant to Fall — 7
2. Join Me in the Arena — 17
3. According to Divine Intelligence — 31
4. Most Earnestly and Persistently — 45
5. Appealing to the Highest Government — 55
6. Living an Innocent Life — 65
7. Anatomy of a Contending House: Part 1 — 73
8. Anatomy of a Contending House: Part 2 — 85
   Other Books by the Authors — 99

CHAPTER 1

GIANTS ARE MEANT TO FALL

Lou Engle

Let us go up at once and take possession, for we are well able to overcome it. (Numbers 13:30)

Being a Contending House of Prayer

"*Our wrestling is not against flesh and blood, but against principalities and powers . . .*" The apostle Paul, in this great Magna Carta of the church in Ephesians 6, gives the key to the outrageous and victorious invasions of Satan's control centers in early New Testament days. If the church in these last days is to fulfill the great commission and establish justice in the earth, then she must renounce fear and fatalism and recover the fierce faith of Paul's frontal attack against the forces of darkness that keep souls bound in the most desperate spiritual and physical captivity. She must return to a wrestling and throwing down of spiritual adversaries in the darkest, hardest places of the earth. God is raising up His house of prayer in the earth to contend with abortion, sex-trafficking, false religions and false ideologies—against every house that exalts itself above the lordship and supremacy of Christ.

In 1996, under the immediacy of God's prophetic direction, we launched a 40-day fast and a 24/7 house of prayer. Our dream was to raise up a Moravian lampstand of prayer, inspired by the hundred year day-and-night prayer meeting of the early Moravians in Eastern Europe that fueled and fired the modern missions movement.

It was in this season of intense prayer and prophetic divine initiative that the Lord gave me my life's job description. In a dream the Lord showed us a Buddhist house of prayer on top of and dominating a Christian house of prayer. Then, suddenly, in this great wrestling match, the Christian house of prayer did a reversal and from a superior position began dominating the Buddhist house of prayer. From this dream, the Lord of Battles gave me my marching orders: Raise up a house of prayer that contends with every other house that exalts itself above the lordship and supremacy of Christ.

Fighting Giants

After forty years of wandering in the wilderness, with an entire generation of warriors never wielding their weapons of war under Moses, Joshua took his place on the stage of Israel's history. By the command of God, he committed a generation to a lifelong war of offensive action and structured the nation into attack formation.

There were no other options. Go die in the wilderness or fight giants in the promised land.

It was in Joshua's day that a new revelation of God was unleashed: the Captain of the Hosts of Heaven (Josh. 5:14). That revelation and command infused a generation with a new attitude: Giants were meant to fall and fortified cities were meant to be captured.

Like Joshua, when the armies of Israel were confronted with the terrorizing taunts of Goliath for forty days and nights, a young warrior David challenged the voices of fear and fatalism with his defiant and pointed question, *"Is there not a cause?"* (1 Sam. 17:29) In that moment, David's voice neither faltered nor hesitated. He knew the battle was the Lord's, and the Lord was seeking occasion to move against the Philistine domination of Israel. God had finally found a man who did not believe negative reports. Goliath's death became the doorway to David's destiny.

One greater than Joshua or David then took His stand on the spiritual battlefield of earth. After thirty years of preparation, He inaugurated the supreme apostolic age by fasting forty days, binding Satan and unleashing His territorial invasion. The result of that heavenly attack was recorded in the Gospel of Matthew, *"And upon those who sat in the region and shadow of death light has dawned."* (4:16) The life job description of this man Jesus was chronicled by John, *"For this purpose the Son of God was manifested, that He might destroy the works of the devil."* (1 John 3:8)

Jesus Himself described His offensive military purpose when He said, *"I will build my church, and the gates of hell* [the powers of death] *will not prevail against it."* (Matt. 16:18) He was committed to establishing His church at the very gates where the powers of darkness and death control the earth and imprison their captives. He would call that church by a name declaring its essential identity as a *"house of prayer for all nations"* (Mark 11:17), and its mandate was to bind and loose in heaven and on earth through agreeing prayer. The house that Jesus builds sets its praying bands at the gates of sex trafficking, abortion, witchcraft, pornography and other outlets of darkness, and they challenge those spiritual forces with the outstretched rod of authoritative prayer in the name of Jesus, saying, "Come down, dark prince!"

This same Jesus, when He defeated principalities and powers at the cross, was raised from the dead and gave a similar commission of offensive spiritual action as Joshua of the Old Testament did with the command of physical war, *"All authority has been given to Me in heaven and earth. Go therefore . . ."* (Matt. 28:18-19) That command was embodied in a supreme way through the apostle Paul who declared to the church, *"The God of peace will crush Satan under your feet shortly."* (Rom. 16:20) The kingdom brings peace through the making of spiritual war. Those New Testament apostles pulled down principalities and powers, attacked the strong man according to Jesus' words and claimed the spoil of souls.

Resisting False Ideologies

What the church needs and what the earth is groaning for now, as we near the end of this apostolic age, are heroic leaders who will follow their Master, who believe that history belongs to the intercessors, and who choose the reality of attack over the rhetoric of peace and acquiescence. Gods wants to raise up a house of prayer movement that will challenge the supreme stranglehold of abortion, which squeezes the life out of our women and their wombs.

God wants a house of prayer that will challenge the slave trades of pornography and every sexual perversion. God wants a house of prayer that will set itself up at the gates of Harvard and every university that espouses and proliferates antichrist philosophies that are discipling a whole generation in a way that leads to death. Ideas have consequences.

It was said that the ovens of Auschwitz were formed in the universities of Europe a hundred years before the Holocaust. Today is no different. 54 million acts of abortion since 1973 were forged by the humanistic philosophies taught in the hallowed halls of Harvard and other institutions. For centuries now, our universities have dictated our destinies and have destroyed and deceived our descendants, but I believe this tyrannical reign of secular humanism can be overthrown. Certainly these giants of humanism and secularism seem overwhelming, yet four men, bound together as a house of prayer, shook the university of Babylon. Daniel and his friends are not an anomaly. They are a prototype of the new breed, the contending house of prayer.

Derek Prince prophesied in 1972 that Boston is the Jericho of America and when the walls of intellectualism come tumbling down, the Lord will pour out His Spirit upon the whole land. It is yet to be seen what a full assault of day and night prayer, extended fasting and laser beam intercession will do to the walls of intellectualism in Boston. In the light of this prophetic word, we have established a contending house of prayer at Harvard, and the reports are coming of a small but significant rumbling. People are gathering. Demons are being driven out. Houses of prayer are rising in the Ivy League schools, and the poison ivy of false ideologies are once again becoming leaves for the healing of the nations.

Many leaders are apprehensive, and understandably so, of challenging the spiritual powers that presently dominate almost every sphere of culture. But I hear a different sound quietly rumbling in this small, weak, but rising prayer movement. Not consumed and overwhelmed by the negative statistics that taunt the church, I can hear the sound of young men or women who refuse to succumb to the counsel of despair and instead are crying, *"Let us go up at once and take possession, for we are well able to overcome it."* (Num. 13:30) Not pacified by the wares of Hollywood or seduced by the fading American dream, there is a divine discontent in the heart of a Nazirite generation with peacefully coexisting with any spirit, ideology or injustice that would try to exalt itself against the knowledge of God.

It is my conviction that we must arm this generation with weapons of fasting, 24/7 prayer, divine prophetic intelligence that penetrates the strong man's armor, and preaching that converts Sauls into Pauls and brings forth paradigm shifts that are really *prayer-adigm* shifts.

The days of prayer meetings to feel good are over. We must pray to win. For people are going to hell, and women are trapped in unbearable human trafficking situations. Those about to die demand a miracle, and a miracle is what the praying church must bring them. Since Roe vs Wade, 54 million babies have been killed in their mother's wombs, and 54 million women have carried guilty wounds.

Battling over the Courts

God sent a company of young people on a mission to do spiritual battle over the Supreme Court where that death decree was made.

Seventy young people prayed continually for fifty days and fifty nights with fasting for a breakthrough. It was a great wrestling match. We needed righteous judges that would be pro-life. Having received guidance through a dream from God, the company was led to stand in front of the Supreme Court building with pieces of LIFE tape over their mouths. God uses the weak things to confound the wise, and the things that are nothing to annul the things that are. It was spiritual war in front of the Supreme Court.

We pleaded the blood of Jesus with LIFE bands on our wrists along with tens of thousands of others across the country praying, "Jesus, I plead your blood over my sins and the sins of my nation. God, end abortion and send revival to America." Day by day young men and women stood lifting up the victory of the cross over the spirit of abortion and death over the Supreme Court. We felt that it was not enough to come to DC and stay for a moment of war.

God wanted a house of prayer at the Supreme Court gate that was committed to stay and siege the powers until Satan bowed to the outstretched rod of prayer.

Furthermore, we needed a building for a house of prayer.

Amazingly, through divinely arranged circumstances, we found a building shaped like an arrowhead and when seen by satellite, points right at the Supreme Court. That building, two blocks from that courthouse, became our staging ground for war. Young people praying night and day by shifts and speaking forth the name of Jesus began to see the prevailing influence over those judges. Breakthroughs began to take place.

Firstly, Chief Justice Rehnquist died during a prayer meeting we were holding. He was a pro-life justice, and we desperately needed a pro-life justice to replace him. When these young people began to prevail in prayer, God began to give them profound prophetic wisdom for battering-ram intercession. One young woman, not knowing anything concerning the potential appointees for this vacancy on the court, had a dream that a man named John Roberts would be the next Supreme Court justice. This word became their focused prayer.

When President George W. Bush came to the moment of appointment, he suddenly changed his mind and appointed John Roberts as the chief justice of the Supreme Court. Don't you think those young people, who had been prevailing in prayer over principalities and powers, were baptized in confidence? They had gained air supremacy over the gates of Sheol, and the powers of death (i.e. abortion) could not prevail. That supremacy was manifested in the raising up and removal of judges. Could angels have been doing their bidding? Clearly the book of Daniel describes the angelic cooperation with human intercession in the changing of times and seasons and the raising up of kings.

In 2001, I was given a profound supernatural calling to pray for Sandra Day O'Connor, a pro-abortion Supreme Court justice. In 2005, Sandra Day O'Connor suddenly and surprisingly resigned from her position. No one expected it. In fact, afterward, she expressed uncertainty and regret for her resignation.

Again divine intelligence was given to this company of prayer showing us that a man from New Jersey would take her place. Just as the Lord had revealed, a man from New Jersey, Justice Samuel Alito, was appointed in her place. The tide had turned. When the horrible and reprehensible practice of late term abortions, that had been previously legalized by the Supreme Court, was brought before this new court, the court was seated, the books were opened, and the decree of death was reversed. The practice of late term abortions was outlawed.

That battle still rages over the Supreme Court to this day, but a company of men and women now six years later still stand with LIFE tape on their mouths in the snow, in the blizzards, and in the heat. Their motto is the quote, "When the victors, when they come, when the forts of folly fall, find my body near the wall." They are saying, "Over my dead body abortion is going to end in America." And that is the true spirit of intercession that overcomes principalities and powers, *"And they overcame him* [Satan] *by the blood of the Lamb and by the word of their testimony, and they did not love their lives unto death."* (Rev. 12:11)

Counting the Cost

To those who read this book, I say—If such drastic changes were unleashed like what happened at the gates of Supreme Court where a contending house of prayer set up its battering rams, then I say there is no safe place for the devil. Every mountain will be brought low.

Let us raise up a house of prayer that contends over Hollywood and makes it "Holywood." Let us raise up a house of prayer in Dearborn, Michigan, that contends for the salvation of Muslims in that city who will come under the dominion of dreams of Jesus and get saved.

Let us raise up a house of prayer in every university where praying radical bands like Daniel and his friends fast, refuse to compromise, and are promoted by divine revelation to the place of preeminence over the pagan professor priests of our temples of humanism. This is no time to live in fear when hostile forces are all about us.

Even nature itself speaks of the divine agenda. When a cancer cell invades a body, a lymphocyte backs up and forms itself in the shape of an arrow and propels itself into that cancer cell destroying it and giving up its own life in the process. Yes, martyrdom will happen when we launch contending prayer strikes and houses of prayer in strongholds of drug lords or in bastions of Islam or Buddhism. But shall we not follow in the path of our Master, saying, *"For the joy set before us we will endure the cross"* (Heb. 12:2)? Like Paul, it is time to raise up a house of prayer that contends with every spiritual power and every house that exalts itself over the lordship and supremacy of Christ.

CHAPTER 2

JOIN ME IN THE ARENA

Sam Cerny

Now I beg you, brethren, through the Lord Jesus Christ, and through the love of the Spirit, that you strive together with me in prayers to God for me. (Romans 15:30)

Imitating Paul

Paul was truly one of the most influential people in all of church history. Of the twenty-eight chapters in Acts, seventeen are primarily about his life and ministry. Of the twenty-seven books in the New Testament, thirteen are written by him. This is not by accident, but by God's design.

God intentionally highlighted Paul in a unique way, but why? Of the thousands upon thousands of Christians in the early church, why Paul? He walked in the way God desires all of His people to walk. He lived as we should all live. He was a pattern for us all. Thus Paul's life is not just to be studied, but also imitated. For Paul himself wrote, "*Imitate me, just as I imitate Christ.*" (1 Cor. 11:1)

Moreover, Paul did not just start well, but also finished well. He fulfilled his destiny to the fullest before he died. He was successful over the course of his entire Christian life. Just before his beheading in Rome, Paul declared, *"The time of my departure is at hand. I have fought the good fight. I have finished the race. I have kept the faith."* (2 Tim. 4:6-7)

Given these realities, we want to learn the keys to Paul's success, of which there are many. Clearly, though, one of these is his prayer life. To live as Paul lived, we must pray as Paul prayed. Was not Paul sharing a key to his own life when he entreated the church to *"pray without ceasing"* (1 Thess. 5:17)?

So let us not just consider that Paul prayed often, but also how he prayed. He did not just pray for personal blessings, but he contended in prayer for collective breakthroughs. As we look at his own writings, we find a man who won battle after battle through praying corporately (Rom. 15:30), intelligently (Eph. 6:18), persistently (1 Thess. 3:9-11), effectively (1 Tim. 2:1-2), and innocently (Rom. 16:19-20). So let us now consider the first of these, that of praying corporately.

The Appeal

"Now I beg you, brethren, through the Lord Jesus Christ, and through the love of the Spirit." (Rom. 15:30)

Paul begins Romans 15:30 with a strong, emotional appeal where he literally begs his brethren to do what he is about to ask. Other versions translate it as *"I urge you, brothers"* (NIV[1]) or *"I appeal to you, brothers"* (ESV[2]). In this he is showing the urgency and priority of what he is about to say. Yet Paul does not stop with just begging them, but he also bases his appeal on two realities.

Firstly, he appeals to the highest of authorities: *"Through the Lord Jesus Christ."* In other words, this plea is not just coming from Paul, but from Jesus. This was not just Paul's

---

1   *New International Version* (International Bible Society, 1973, 1978, 1984)

2   *English Standard Version* (Crossway Bibles, a division of Good New Publishers, 2001)

idea, but God's command. To ignore it is to ignore the Lord.

Secondly, he appeals to the highest of motivations: *"Through the love of the Spirit."* Love is the one motivation that lasts when all others fade away, for love *"endures all things. Love never fails."* (1 Cor. 13:7-8) The word used is *agape* which defines the type of love referred to, as there are multiple words in Greek referencing different types of love. With *phileo* (brotherly love) or *eros* (romantic love), people are loved because they bring pleasure to others. In this way, family members, friends, and spouses can be loved. Such can have a selfish motivation, though. With *agape* (godly love), people are loved because they are precious to others. In this way, even enemies or more difficult people can be loved. Such can only have a selfless motivation. So through appealing to the love of the Spirit, Paul is asking the Roman church to consider the preciousness of the people who are reached through his and their ministries. The church is to love them as the Spirit loves them.

What, though, is Paul begging them to do? What had such an urgency? What had such a high priority?

The Arena

". . . that you strive together with me . . ." (Rom. 15:30)

Paul appeals to them to *"strive together,"* but what does that mean? This phrase is a translation of the Greek word *sunagonidzomai*, which is a combination of *sun*, meaning together or in union, and *agonidzomai*, meaning to contend with an adversary or struggle with an opponent. It is from the root word *agon* meaning a place of assembly or contest, and it refers to the Roman arenas or coliseums where gladiators fought and wrestled or where athletes fought to overcome and win the prize.

Thus, this verb *agonidzomai* is usually translated as "fight," and some of those examples include: *"Jesus answered, 'My kingdom is not of this world. If My kingdom were of this world, My servants would fight (agonidzomai)."'* (John 18:36) *"Epaphras, who is one of you and a servant of Christ Jesus, sends greetings. He is always wrestling (agonidzomai) in prayer for you . . . "* (Col. 4:12 NIV) *"Fight (agonidzomai) the good fight of faith."* (1 Tim. 6:12) So other translations of Romans 15:30 include *"be my allies in the fight"* (NEB[3]) and "join me in my struggle. " (NIV)

What does Paul's use of this verb imply? Fighting implies that there are opponents, and in Paul's case, he and the churches were constantly opposed by the demonic realm. In the very next chapter, Paul wrote in the future tense, *"And the God of peace will crush Satan under your feet shortly"* (Rom. 16:20), which means that satanic resistance was happening at that present time. Consider some of the ways in which Satan had resisted Paul and his apostolic team.

Their preaching was opposed. *"Who was with the proconsul, Sergius Paulus, an intelligent man. This man called for Barnabas and Saul and sought to hear the word of God. But Elymas the sorcerer (for so his name is translated) withstood them* (resisted, opposed), *seeking to turn the proconsul away from the faith. Then Saul, who also is called Paul, filled with the Holy Spirit, looked intently at him and said, 'O full of all deceit and all fraud, you son of the devil, you enemy of all righteousness, will you not cease perverting the straight ways of the Lord?'"* (Acts 13:7-10) In this instance, Paul, Silas, and their preaching were not just withstood by a man, but by a man deeply influenced by Satan and satanic deceptions.

Their praying was disturbed. *"Now it happened, as we went to prayer, that a certain slave girl possessed with a spirit of divination met us, who brought her masters much profit by fortune-telling. This girl followed Paul and us, and cried out, saying, 'These men are the servants of the Most High God,*

---

3   *The New English Bible with the Apocrypha* (Oxford University Press and Cambridge University Press, 1970)

who proclaim to us the way of salvation.' And this she did for many days. But Paul, greatly annoyed [distressed, disturbed], *turned and said to the spirit, 'I command you in the name of Jesus Christ to come out of her.' And he came out that very hour."* (Acts 16:16-18) This mocking demon was greatly annoying, distressing, and disturbing Paul and his team as they sought to go pray.

Their lives and doctrine were attacked. *"Put on the whole armor of God, that you may be able to stand against the wiles* [deceptions, distortions] *of the devil. For we do not wrestle against flesh and blood, but against principalities, against powers, against the rulers of the darkness of this age, against spiritual hosts of wickedness in the heavenly places."* (Eph. 6:11-12) This word translated as *"wiles"* carries the sense of distortion or deception, and so this same term is translated as *"deceitful plotting"* in Ephesians 4:14. Again and again, Paul's teachings were undermined in instances like *"contradicting and blaspheming, they opposed the things spoken by Paul"* (Acts 13:45), *"and poisoned their minds against the brethren"* (14:2), and *"having persuaded the multitudes, they stoned Paul and dragged him out of the city."* (14:19)

Their ministry travels and agendas were hindered. *"Therefore we wanted to come to you, even I Paul, time and again—but Satan hindered* [stopped, impeded] *us."* (1 Thess. 2:18) Paul understood that he was not just stopped by circumstances, but by Satan.

Again, think about 1 Thessalonians 2:18. Paul was one of the most obedient and mature Christians who ever lived, yet Satan was able to stop him for a season. If Satan could stop Paul, then he can stop us. Whether or not this verse fits our theology, it is reality.

However, Paul did not accept demonic resistance as inevitable or unalterable. Rather he knew how to rightly respond. So how did he react? What did he do?

The Attack

"*. . . in your prayers to God far me . . .*" (Rom. 15:30)

First and foremost, this battle is engaged "*in prayers,*" and so this conflict is played out in the invisible realms or heavenly planes. As Paul and the Ephesian church wrestled against demonic powers in heavenly places (Eph. 6:11-13), they were "*praying always with all prayer and supplication in the Spirit, being watchful to this end with all perseverance and supplication for all the saints.*" (6:18). As Paul and his team were hindered by Satan from visiting the church in Thessalonica (1 Thess. 2:18), they were "*night and day praying exceedingly that we may see your face and perfect what is lacking in your faith.*" (3:10}

However, Romans 15:30 is not just a description of Paul praying, but an appeal from Paul for the church to pray with him and for him. Paul understood that to an extent his destiny was dependent on their prayers. What God called Paul to do he could not accomplish individually, but only corporately. Thus like Paul, we are forced not just to be dependent on God, but on one another as well. This is by God's design and can be clearly seen in Paul's words to the church in Corinth: "*Yes, we had the sentence of death in ourselves, that we should not trust in ourselves but in God who raises the dead, who delivered us from so great a death, and does deliver us; in whom we trust that He will still deliver us, you also helping together in prayer for us, that thanks may be given by many persons on our behalf for the gift granted to us through many.*" (2 Cor. 1:9-11)

The Agreement

"*That you strive together with me in your prayers to God far me.*" (Rom. 15:30}

Furthermore, Romans 15:30 is not just about praying together, but about agreeing in prayer together. This word *sunagonidzomai* refers to being in unity and harmony. Consider the unity within a company of soldiers fighting for each other on the battlefield. It refers to having a lack of strife and division. It denotes being in agreement in regards to each other's purposes, commitments, attitudes, beliefs, and so forth. It involves being in agreement relationally, not just doctrinally. Earlier on in chapter 15, Paul highlighted this when he penned, *"May the God who gives endurance and encouragement give you a spirit of unity among yourselves as you follow Christ Jesus, so that with one heart and mouth you may glorify the God and Father of our Lord Jesus Christ."* (Rom. 15:5-6 NIV)

Jesus also emphasized this same point when teaching on prayer, for He declared, *"Again, I say to you that if two of you agree on earth concerning anything that they ask, it will be done for them by my Father in heaven."* (Matt. 18:19) It it not enough just to ask, for we must also agree. Yet what type of agreement is Jesus describing?

In Greek, this word *"agree"* is *symphoneo*, from which our English word symphony is derived. It is a combination of *sun*, meaning together or in union, and *phone*, meaning voice or sound. In a symphony, how do the various musicians, instruments, and singers flow together? How are those sounds in accordance with each other? For those musicians, much preparation, effort, and focus go into not breaking the unity of sounds.

So in Matthew 18:19 *symphoneo* implies having a harmonious relationship, not just intellectual agreement. It indicates profound harmony on the level of each other's commitments, attitudes, motivations, and so on. Peter used this same word when portraying Sapphira's agreement with her husband Ananias: *"Then Peter said to her, 'How is it that you have agreed together (symphoneo) to test the Spirit of the Lord? Look, the feet of those who have buried your husband are at the door, and they will carry you out.'"* (Acts 5:9) What kind of agreement was needed for them to commit to a plan to scheme, lie, and resist the apostles and even God Himself? How strong was their agreement? For that couple, such an agreement was held even to the point of death!

Moreover, Matthew 18:19 begins with the word "again", which is used in the sense of repetition. Jesus is actually repeating and expanding on what he just said. In the previous verse, He was speaking about the authority of the church and said, "*Assuredly, I say to you, whatever you bind on earth will be bound in heaven, and whatever you loose on earth will be loosed in heaven.*" (Matt. 18:18, also in 16:19)

This statement in both Matthew 18:18 and 16:19 is a depiction of the church's high calling as both verses immediately follow the only two references to the church in the gospels (Matt. 18:17, 16:18). In other words, Jesus would not introduce the church without introducing her calling. What the church binds or looses from earth is restricted or released in heaven. There is a direct connection between what happens on earth and what happens in heaven.

In regard to the authority of the church, both realms are affected.

Scripturally, these verbs *"bind"* (Gr. *deo*) and *"loose"* (Gr. *luo*) mean to restrict and release. On a physical level, they refer to tying up or freeing animals or people (Matt. 21:2, John 11:44, Acts 12:6). On a spiritual level, they are connected to the activity of angels or demons (Matt. 12:28-29, Luke 13:16, Rev. 9:14-15), which are moved in response to the church's words and works.

Yet how does the church do the binding and loosing of Matthew 18:18? How does the church exercise her authority depicted in this verse? Through the agreeing and asking of 18:19. "*Whatever you bind on earth . . . whatever you loose on earth*" (18:18) is explained further with "*If two of you agree on earth concerning anything that they ask*" (18:19). "*Will be bound in heaven . . . will be loosed in heaven*" (18:18) is expounded further with "*It will be done for them by My Father in heaven*" (18:19).

How, though, is this agreement maintained? Understanding the implications of Jesus' words in Matthew 18:18-20, Peter ponders how to live out this teaching and asks, "*Lord, how often shall my brother sin against me, and I forgive him?*

Up to seven times?" (Matt. 18:21) Jesus' answer is a key to maintaining such agreement: *"I do not say to you, up to seven times, but up to seventy times seven."* (18:22)

How far do we go to preserve this unity? In other words, how often do you have to forgive a brother, friend, or coworker who keeps sinning against you in small or large ways? What about the friend who keeps gossiping behind your back? What about those critical comments from the other worship team member? What about the brother in the Lord who keeps showing up late and doesn't respect your time? What about the fellow Bible college student who keeps boasting about how devoted and anointed she is? When someone keeps sinning against you or annoying you constantly, how should you respond? What did Jesus say?

Your only response should be forgiveness, which is not counting their sins against them. Forgiveness means you don't criticize them in return. You don't try to justify yourself and tear them down at the same time. You don't keep a record of their faults. You don't let everyone else know how they failed.

If you were truly harmed by a person's words or actions, then forgiveness includes following the steps of Matthew 18:15-17. These steps are not a means to show your friends or church leaders how right you are and how wrong they are. Instead, they are a safe way for you to express honesty, humility and forgiveness to the other person, whether or not the other person responds rightly.

Jesus told Peter not just to forgive the other person seven times, but four hundred and ninety times! In essence, we need to forgive others in the same way the Lord has forgiven us. Certainly, He's forgiven us countless times! From the cross, He even forgave those who falsely accused, mocked, stripped, humiliated, beat, whipped, and crucified Him. *"Father, forgive them, for they do not know what they do."* (Luke 23:34)

In order to truly have authority in prayer, we need to have agreement among ourselves. In order to have agreement among ourselves, we need to follow Paul's exhortation to be continually *"bearing with one another, and forgiving one another, if anyone has a complaint against another; even as Christ forgave you, so you also must do."* (Col. 3:13)

While on a prayer expedition to Mount Kailash in western Tibet in 1994, my friend Jamie and I experienced first-hand the truths of Romans 15:30 and Matthew 18:19. The following is that account.

Exerting Christ's Authority

For the approximately 900 million Hindus, 400 million Buddhists, and 5 million Jainists, Mount Kailash is considered the most holy place in the universe. The four faces of its icy, pyramidal cone face exactly the four directions of north, south, east, and west. From its surrounding region are the headwaters of four major rivers that water the Tibetan plateau and Indian subcontinent.

Kailash is encircled by altars, shrines, meditation caves, and Buddhist monasteries, and each year tens of thousands of pilgrims walk around the mountain with some of them prostrating the entire way. They believe such a pilgrimage will shed the sins of past lives and help speed them to enlightenment. Furthermore, Hindus believe that Kailash is the throne of their goddess Shiva, while Buddhists believe it is the dwelling of Demchok, a supreme deity in their pantheon of gods. They also believe it is the earthly manifestation of Mount Meru, a cosmic world mountain around which all the universe revolves. It is considered the naval of the universe. Many famous Buddhist saints are also said to have achieved enlightenment in the shadow of this mountain. In summary, the region of Mount Kailash is truly one of the darkest demonic strongholds on earth.

I had been living in Lhasa, Tibet, as a student of Tibet University for a year when the summer of '94 arrived. From that capital city in central Tibet, my friend Jamie and I traveled to the far edges of Ngari, the westernmost prefecture on that Himalayan plateau. Our aim was to pray, worship, and share Christ among the nomad encampments, villages, and Buddhist monasteries throughout that distant, rugged land. Mount Kailash, though, was our ultimate destination.

After driving for eight days, we arrived at the village of Toling, which lies amidst massive canyons akin to the Grand Canyon in the United States. The arid desert landscape enveloped by massive canyon walls was breathtaking to view. Toling itself was centered around a large, aged Buddhist monastery, and on its outskirts stood ancient pyramid-like altars. High up on the canyon walls meditation caves could be seen. We were only a two-day drive from Kailash.

During our first night in that village, we began to sing praise songs and worship Jesus in our small guesthouse room. It was furnished in Tibetan fashion, and its walls were brushed with bright colors. Within minutes of singing, my mind was filled with hideous images of various Tibetan deities, and my heart felt oppressed. The taunt of the enemy continued for quite a while. We felt to continue singing, and so we did. At one point, that sense of evil oppression lifted as the presence of the Lord rushed in with great power. My hands felt like they were literally burning with electricity as the Spirit blanketed us. It turned into a glorious night of praise.

From Toling we drove to the hot springs of Tradapuri, which is a very sacred site for Buddhists. Centuries earlier, a famous Buddhist saint meditated in a cave near those springs and performed many miracles. Around the springs and cave was a circular pilgrimage path that Buddhists walked daily. Nearly a torrential river flowed, and beyond it towered the snow-capped peaks of the Himalayas. We were only one day from Kailash.

That night we slept in our Toyota Landcruiser in the middle of a vast field near the springs, and the next morning we woke up just as the sun's light shot over the horizon. Peering out the windows, we saw a man walking towards us. He arrived at our car, walked to each side, flicked his fingers, spoke some chants, and then walked away. We believed he was performing some kind of sorcery. At that moment, Jamie lost his ability to see clearly with his eyes. Suddenly, we both became very anxious and asked God for help. What should we do? How should we respond to this particular demonic attack? Without a doubt, we suddenly knew what the Lord's strategy was.

Stepping out of the Landcruiser, we grabbed Jamie's guitar and began walking to the Buddhist pilgrimage path nearby. We strongly sensed from the Spirit that we were to walk the entire route and pray and worship at four key points along it. We arrived at the path and ascended up to its highest point, and as we walked, Jamie's vision was restored. At the uppermost point, we knelt down next to a large Buddhist altar full of stones with prayers carved on them, bones, and other ritual objects. From the top of the altar were strung many colorful flags with Buddhist prayers written on them.

At that spot, we started praising the Lord and sang in English and in tongues. Soon waves of God's glory started cascading upon us. His presence was so near, as if we were in heaven directly before His throne. Again, my hands and arms burned as with fire and electricity.

Tibetan pilgrims gathered around and watched as we worshiped. It was one of the greatest worship services I had ever been in, and that right in one of the spiritually darkest places on the planet!

Afterward, we drove to Kailash. The next morning we started on our three-day hike along the circular pilgrimage path around the mountain. As we walked, we prayed in the Spirit, sang worship songs, and asked for God's kingdom to come. High above us towered the snowy, icy face of Kailash. Around us waterfalls plunged down from rocky ridges, and flowery meadows draped the valleys.

However, while nature's beauty and serenity surrounded us, my heart was anything but serene.

As we hiked, my mind became inundated with accusations, condemnation, and lies. As Jamie continued singing, I found myself annoyed with the sound of his voice. Then I started remembering past difficult situations with him, and though I had not been bothered before, suddenly resentments started flaring up. I began despising almost everything about him. I knew these were not just my thoughts, but accusations from the enemy. I felt powerless over them, though. These demonic voices began telling me that my friendship with Jamie, my closest friend, would be destroyed by the end of this journey. Tension between us appeared to be mounting, and we were hardly talking to each other after a while.

By the time we reached our campsite at the convergence of two stunning mountain streams, the accusations, oppression, and depression were so heavy that I wanted to run from that place. I wanted to immediately flee the Kailash region. After setting up camp and eating dinner, nightfall came, and we retreated into our tent. Sitting inside, I told Jamie about everything I had experienced that day. He too had felt the same way. We both wept and asked the Lord for His strategy for dealing with this seemingly overwhelming assault.

Immediately, we knew what to do. Something more than prayer or praise was needed. We reaffirmed our friendship by making a David and Jonathan covenant before the Lord (1 Sam. 18:1-4). I said to Jamie that everything I own was his, my time was his, and if he ever needed me at any time, I would go to him even if it was across the ocean. He reciprocated the same commitments to me.

Following that, we entered into an extraordinary time of worship and praise, and the manifest presence of God filled our tent. I remember distinctly feeling like His Spirit was falling like rain upon us. We then proceeded into intense intercession for Tibet.

Over the next few days, some significant doors opened for the gospel. We were able to pass out worship music tapes to pilgrims, present the gospel of Mark in the Tibetan language to an old monk living in a small, remote monastery, share the gospel and pray with a Navy SEAL team from Singapore who were visiting Kailash on a spiritual pilgrimage, and see God's hand move in miraculous ways.

Over the next few years, larger breakthroughs occurred in other Tibetan regions as well. For us, we saw that once we reached a place of greater agreement and unity, greater authority and power in Christ were released.

CHAPTER 3

ACCORDING TO DIVINE INTELLIGENCE

Sam Cerny

> *Praying always with all prayer and supplication in the Spirit, being watchful to this end with all perseverance and supplication for all the saints.*
> (Ephesians 6:18)

Unconquerable Power

"*Finally; my brethren, be strong in the Lord and in the power of His might.*" (Eph. 6:10)

Near the end of his letter to the Ephesian church, Paul exhorts them to walk in the might and power of the Lord. However, near the beginning of the letter, he introduces them to the Lord's might and power as that which raised Christ from the dead. "*And what is the exceeding greatness of His power toward us who believe, according to the working of His mighty power which He worked in Christ when He raised Him from the dead and seated Him at His right hand in the heavenly places.*" (Eph. 1:19-20)

The apostles fully understood this resurrection power. With their eyes they saw Christ alive in His resurrected body, though He had died. Paul also saw Him (1 Cor. 15:8). For them, that display of power resulted in the defeat of death, the last and final enemy. There was no doubt in their minds that through the Lord's might and power every enemy will be conquered, whether the battle be short or long. This is the same mighty power that Paul encourages the church to experience in Ephesians 6:10. If we walk in it, the defeat of our enemies is certain. Along these same lines, Jesus said, "I saw Satan fall like lightning from heaven. Behold, I give you the authority to trample on serpents and scorpions, and over all the power of the enemy . . ." (Luke 10:18-19)

As a man of fiery prayer and evangelism, Charles Finney helped spark one of the greatest spiritual awakenings ever in America, and he too experienced that unconquerable power of God in the place of intercession. Regarding that, he wrote, "I found myself so much I exercised and so borne down with the weight of immortal souls, that I was constrained to pray without ceasing. Some of my experiences indeed alarmed me. A spirit of importunity sometimes came upon me so that I would pray to God that He had made a promise to answer prayer and I could not and would not be denied. I felt myself so certain that He would hear me that frequently I found myself saying to Him: 'I hope Thou dost not think that I can be denied. I come with Thy faithful promises in my hand, and I will not be denied.' My impression was that the answer was very near, even at the door; and *I felt myself strengthened in the Divine life, put on the harness for a mighty conflict with the powers of darkness* and expected soon to see a far more powerful outpouring of the Spirit of God. Nor did God disappoint this praying disciple, for larger spheres of spiritual usefulness were soon to open."[1]

So why does Paul give this exhortation in Ephesians 6:10? Because of the war described in 6:11-12, which is a war we are already in.

---

1 Miller, Basil, *Charles Finney* (Minneapolis: Bethany House, 1941), pp. 50-51

The Resistance Movement

"Put on the whole armor of God, that you may be able to stand against the wiles of the devil. For we do not wrestle against flesh and blood, but against principalities, against powers, against the rulers of the darkness of this age, against spiritual hosts of wickedness in the heavenly places." (Eph. 6:11-12)

When facing the *"wiles of the devil,"* we should not be ignorant, indifferent, or passive. Instead, we need to *"stand against"* them. This is a stance of resisting, not accepting. It is a stance of pushing back, not running from.

This word "wiles" is *methodeia* meaning craftiness, trickery, deceit, or distortion. Any ideology not based on truth needs to be resisted. Any deceptive doctrine of demons needs to be pushed back. This could include false belief systems like evolution or humanism, false religions like Mormonism or Islam, or false doctrines within the church itself. About these types of false ideologies and deceptive arguments, Paul wrote, *"For the weapons of our warfare are not carnal but mighty in God for pulling down strongholds, casting down arguments and every high things that exalts itself against the knowledge of God."* (2 Cor. 10:4-5)

When facing *"principalities,"* *"powers,"* *"rulers of the darkness of this age,"* and *"spiritual hosts of wickedness"* in *"the heavenly places,"* we should not be fearful, timid, or apathetic. Instead, we need to *"wrestle against"* them. This word *"wrestle"* is pale which refers to *"a contest between two till one hurls the other down and holds him down."*[2] It is from the root word *pallo* which means to throw off or cast down.

The early church did not cower in the face of darkness, but rather pushed it back again and again. In this context

---

2   Robertson, A.M., D.D., LLD., Litt. D., Archibald Thomas, *Word Pictures in the New Testament* (The Sunday School Board of the Southern Baptist Convention, 1933, Renewal 1960)

of spiritual warfare, consider the combative verbs they used: "*crush*" (Rom. 16:20), "*pulling down . . . casting down*" (2 Cor. 10:4-5), "*standing against . . . wrestling against*" (Eph. 6:11-12), "*resist*"(James 4:7), and "*overcome*" (1 John 2:13).

Furthermore, though the battlefield is in the invisible realm, these are genuine battles which Paul is describing. These are real wrestling matches which may require real blood, sweat, and tears. However, we do not stand against satanic ideologies or wrestle against demonic authorities in order to gain the victory, but rather to enforce the victory already gained. Through Christ's crucifixion, resurrection, and ascension, He was seated "*at His right hand in the heavenly places, far above all principality and power and might and dominion, and every name that is named, not only in this age but also in that which is to come.*" (Eph. 1:20-21) At the cross, Christ "*disarmed principalities and powers*" and "*made a public spectacle of them, triumphing over them in it.*" (Col 2:15)

In Christ, we too sit with Him in heavenly places and share in His victory over principalities and powers, for He "*raised us up together, and made us sit together in the heavenly places in Christ Jesus.*"

(Eph. 2:6) Again, Paul reminds us, "*And you are complete in Him, who is the head of all principality and power.*" (Col. 2:10) Our position in Him, though, should not lead us into apathy, but into combat.

Thus in this age, we have both overcome and are still overcoming. We are victorious and are still seeing that victory being worked out. While the war has been won, many battles are still to be fought. So practically how do we stand against the wiles of the devil? How do we wrestle against these powers of darkness? Part of that answer is laid out in the following verses in Ephesians 6:13-18.

Our Weapons

"*And take the sword of the Spirit, which is the word of God; praying always with all prayer and supplication in the*

Spirit, being watchful to this end with all perseverance and supplication for all the saints." (Eph. 6:17-18)

In Ephesians 6:13-17, Paul talks about the defensive armor we need to wear, for as we enter these conflicts, very real *"fiery darts of the wicked one"* (6:16) will be shot in our direction. These could entail accusations (Zech. 3:1, Matt. 4:3-10, Rev. 12:10), deceptions (John 8:44, Acts 13:10, 2 Cor. 11:13-15, 1 Tim. 4:1), temptations (Matt. 6:13, 1 Cor. 7:5, 1 Thess. 3:5), persecutions (2 Thess. 3:2-3, Rev. 2:10), and other types of attacks (1 Peter 5:8-9, Rev. 12:17).

Backlash and retaliation from the enemy are very real, but at the same time, protection and covering from the Lord are very real as well. We are not told just to take up armor, but *"the whole armor of God."* (6:11, 13) This is God's armor, the very armor He clothes Himself in as described in passages like Isaiah 11:5 and 59:17. The Lord's armor, though, is not just fanciful imagery, metaphor, or an ethereal and abstract idea. It is His character, the way He lives, which we can *"put on"* (6:11) and live in. It is walking in His truth (6:14), righteousness (6:14), peace (6:15), faith (6:16), and salvation (6:17).

It is because Christ as a man fully clothed Himself with this armor and walked in this lifestyle that He could say, *"The ruler of this world is coming, and he has nothing in me."* (John 14:30) This does not mean that Christ did not suffer, but that He was not conquered. Not one fiery dart pierced Him. Satan gained no foothold in Him.

In Ephesians 6:17-18, Paul then lists two offensive weapons to be wielded. The first is *"the sword of the Spirit, which is the word of God,"* and the second is *"all prayer and supplication in the Spirit."* Regarding the first, it is the proclamation of God's words, which could entail declaring the gospel, preaching the Scriptures, or speaking prophetic words. The key, though, is that it is the sword *"of the Spirit."* This is not just speaking right words, but words initiated by the Spirit in the moment. Thus, in this battle Paul asks *"that utterance may be given me."* (6:19) During His own conflict with Satan,

Jesus spoke of living *"by every word that proceeds from the mouth of God."*(Matt. 4:4)

The second is prayers to God, but likewise, these are not just prayers, but prayers *"in the Spirit."* It is one thing to pray to God, but another to pray with Him. These are prayers initiated by the Spirit in the moment. To more fully understand how to be triumphant in these battles, we need to more fully understand what it means to pray in the Spirit. What did Paul mean by this phrase? How did Paul pray in the Spirit? Why is this so crucial in spiritual warfare?

To answer that, we must look at Paul's writings related to this, for in them we learn how and why we should pray in the Spirit. With the Spirit, we will pray according to His thoughts (Rom. 8:26-27), affections (Gal. 4:6), intentions (Gal. 4:19), and strategies (Eph. 6:18). In other words, we pray intelligently. Without gathering intelligence from an agency like the CIA, a military campaign will not be successful. In the same way, without praying intelligently, we may not be effective.

According to His Mind

"Likewise the Spirit also helps in our weaknesses. For we do not know what we should pray for as we ought, but the Spirit Himself makes intercession for us with groanings which cannot be uttered. Now He who searches the hearts knows what the mind of the Spirit is, because He makes intercession for the saints according to the will of God." (Rom. 8:26-27)

According to Romans 8:26, how does the Spirit pray through us?

"With groans that words cannot express." (NIV) This word *"groans"* is *stegnamos* meaning to groan or sigh deeply. It implies expressing ideas, emotions, and desires of the Spirit that cannot be expressed with human words. There is no language to truly portray what is on His mind, heart, and will.

According to Romans 8:27, why does the Spirit pray through us? *"Because He makes intercession for the saints according to the will of God."* Though God is all-sovereign, at times He chooses to release or I withhold His will based on our prayers. That is why we pray, *"Your will be done on earth as it is in heaven."* (Matt. 6:10)

So it is critical not just that we pray, but that we pray according to His will. *"Now this is the confidence that we have in Him, that if we ask anything according to His will, He hears us."* (1 John 5:14) However, the problem is that in many situations we do not know what God's will is, and we do not know what to pray for. "For we do not know what we should pray for as we ought." (Rom. 8:26) Thus we need the Spirit to pray through us, for He fully comprehends God's mind, heart, and will. *"Now He who searches the hearts knows what the mind of the Spirit is."* (8:27) Given this reality, only the Spirit has the intelligence and targets we need in prayer.

According to His Affections

And because you are sons, God has sent forth the Spirit of His Son into your hearts, crying out, *"Abba, Father!"* (Gal 4:6)

According to Galatians 4:6, how does the Spirit pray through us? He is *"crying out."*—This verb is *kradzo* meaning to cry aloud, scream, or shriek. It is "used especially of the 'cry' of a raven; then, of any inarticulate cries."[3] It infers speaking from passion, not just from information. In a corporate office, people usually talk in a normal tone and very matter-of-factly. Why? Because they are merely relaying information and facts. In a football game or rock concert, people usually scream and shout. Why? Because they are relaying passion and excitement.

According to Galatians 4:6, why does the Spirit pray through us?

---

3   Vine, William E., *Vine's Expository Dictionary of Old and New Testament Words*, (W.E Vine, 1940)

So that we can cry out *"Abba, Father!"* This is a statement of deep intimacy. The title "Father" is more formal while the title *"Abba"* is much more personal. It is the equivalent of calling God "Daddy" in English!

In ancient Jewish households, servants or slaves were allowed to call the head of the household "Father," but they were forbidden to call him *"Abba."* Such a title was only reserved for one's own children, as it was a personal, relational, and intimate word. The implication is that when we pray in the Spirit, we are led into a close intimacy with the Father. Thus our relationship with God is not just kneeling before a King on His throne, but also sitting on the lap of our Father.

About this, Paul wrote, *"For through Him we both have access by one Spirit to the Father"*(Eph. 2:18) In regard to intimately approaching the Father (*"to the Father"*), there are two truths in his verse: Firstly, Jesus provides the right of access (*"for through Him"*). When He died on the cross, what happened to the veil in the temple separating the outer courts and the inner sanctuary where the presence of God dwelt? It was torn from top to bottom to prove that God, not man, tore it (Matt. 27:50-51). Jesus' death made a way for us to enter the presence of the Father. However, given that truth, why do so many still not draw near to Him?

Secondly, the Spirit provides the power of access (*"by one Spirit"*). Christ opened the way, but the Spirit carries us in. Jesus provided legal access, but the Spirit provides experiential access. So praying in the Spirit is a means to entering in.

According to His Intentions

"My little children, for whom I labor in birth again until Christ is formed in you." (Gal. 4:19)

According to Galatians 4:19, how does the Spirit pray through us? *"My little children, of whom I travail in birth . . ."* (KJV) This phrase *"travail in birth"* is the Greek word *odino* meaning to travail or feel the pains of childbirth.

Elsewhere in Scripture, this word is used only two other times in Galatians 4:27 and Revelation 12:2, where it is translated, *"She was pregnant and cried out in pain (odino) as she was about to give birth."* (Rev. 12:2 NIV)

According to Galatians 4:19, why does the Spirit pray through us? So that the life of Christ can be birthed in others. So that Christ can be *"formed"* in them.

Notice that Paul inserts the word *"again"* in this verse. He understood that these formerly pagan idolaters (Gal. 4:8-9) were initially brought to Christ through travailing prayer. He initially helped birth them into God's family through intense intercession, and he even calls them *"my little children"*, which implies having helped birth them.

However, by this point, these Christians were ready to reject Christ and embrace the religion of the Pharisees. *"I marvel that you are turning away so soon from Him who called you in the grace of Christ, to a different gospel . . ."* (Gal. 1:6) So Paul entered again into the same travailing prayer that first led them to encounter and turn to Christ, but this time so that they would re-encounter and return to Him. *"For whom I labor in birth again . . ."* (4:19)

According to His Strategies

"Praying always with all prayer and supplication in the Spirit, being watchful to this end with all perseverance and supplication for all the saints." (Eph. 6:18)

According to Ephesians 6:18, how does the Spirit pray through us? *"And pray in the Spirit on all occasions with all kinds of prayer and requests."* (NIV) This phrase *"all kinds"* implies many different types of praying in the Spirit, for it can include any kind of prayer initiated by or under the unction of the Spirit. Those types can entail speaking in tongues, singing in tongues, groaning, crying out, travailing, or praying with prophetic insight from dreams, visions, impressions, highlighted verses, or other means. All of these ways can be found in Scripture.

Regarding speaking in tongues specifically, we must remember that this was a primary activity in Paul's life. Consider how much time he spent doing this if he was able to honestly say, "*I thank God that I speak in tongues more than you all.*" (1 Cor. 14:18)

According to Ephesians 6:18, why does the Spirit pray through us? In context, so that we can "*stand against the wiles of the devil*" (6:11) and "*wrestle against . . . principalities, against powers, against the rulers of darkness of this age, against spiritual hosts of wickedness in the heavenly places.*" (6:12) Ephesians 6:10-18 is about spiritual warfare, and the final, climactic point in this section is to be "praying always . . . in the Spirit." (6:18) Such praying results in God's answers being released and His enemies being restricted. Both happen when we pray in the Spirit.

Throughout the Scriptures, we read that verbal declarations from God push back and bind His enemies. Notice in the following verse how God's crying out and shouting aloud are linked to His prevailing over His enemies: "*The Lord shall go forth like a mighty man; He shall stir up His zeal like a man of war. He shall cry out, yes, shout aloud; He shall prevail against His enemies.*" (Isa. 42:13)

So when we pray in the Spirit, at times we are joining the war cry of the Lord, and demonic beings are resisted. In other words, His shout of victory becomes our shout of victory, and satanic assignments are canceled. "*The LORD his God is with him, and the shout of a King is among them. God brings them out of Egypt; He has strength like a wild ox. For there is no sorcery against Jacob, nor any divination against Israel. It now must be said of Jacob and of Israel, 'Oh, what God has done!'*" (Num. 23:21-23)

Overcoming the Enemy

Twice in my life I attended Discipleship Training Schools hosted by Youth With A Mission. In 1993 I attended a DTS in Pune, India, as a single man, and then in 1998 my wife and I joined a DTS in Harpenden, England, as a newly married couple. Both times I had life-changing encounters in regards to praying in the Spirit and overcoming the enemy.

While in Pune, one night I had a dream. In it I saw the son of one of the school leaders, who was a young boy from Sri Lanka who had been adopted by this Dutch couple. He was being tormented by a demon, and it literally looked like invisible fists were beating his face and body. I could see the impact of each hit. I then laid my hands on his chest and started rebuking this tormenter and speaking in tongues.

Suddenly, I awoke from the dream, and I was sitting up in my bed literally speaking in tongues with great fervency. My Indian roommate woke up alarmed, but I told him everything was okay and to go back to sleep. Sensing that I was not yet finished, I walked outside into the cool night air and paced back and forth on the veranda praying in the Spirit.

The next morning I was hesitant to share this with the leader, since I knew nothing about his son. I had no knowledge of any struggles he was or was not having. Yet I did end up telling him about the previous night's experience, and he was grateful for what happened. He said that his son never mentioned Jesus but did refer to the devil as his friend. This had been a cause of concern for him and his wife.

The next day, this leader approached me and excitedly said that a real breakthrough had occurred in his son's relationship with Jesus.

For the first time, his son told him that Jesus was his friend, and this was of his own initiative. There was a noticeable change in his son's heart.

Years later in 1998 my wife and I were students at the YWAM school in Harpenden, England. The school was held at a quaint English residence called Highfield Oval which had extensive green lawns, red brick buildings, and a lovely stone chapel. Each week a different guest lecturer would come and share. During the third week in June, the speaker was from the YWAM base in Amsterdam, and for years she had been ministering to prostitutes in the infamous red-light district of that city.

One afternoon, as a group we spent time waiting on the Lord. At one point, we gathered around the speaker and started praying for her. Then, suddenly, God's presence rested on me so heavily that I collapsed to the floor. It felt like fire rushing over me. Others too fell under the weight of His presence. From deep within our hearts flowed prayers without words, and we groaned and wept.

Then in a vision I was looking over the city of Amsterdam, and I saw an angel standing over the city with a spear-like weapon in its hand.[4] I caught a glimpse of the Lord's indescribable power and authority, and I started trembling. In that moment, I sensed the Spirit releasing a loud cry or shout from within me. I felt like I was to declare the authority of Christ over Amsterdam, and no words can adequately express such omnipotent power. So about four times I unleashed a loud, roaring shout.

That summer we finished the YWAM school and returned to America. In October, I called my brother who had been ministering full-time in Amsterdam, for he and I had not spoken with each other since before our DTS in England. He proceeded to tell me about many spiritual breakthroughs that had recently occurred there. He said that since earlier that year many young people had come to Jesus, and their youth ministry had really grown. He started leading a Bible study in the basement of the building and called it the "Living Room," where they would worship, pray, and share simple Bible studies out of the gospels. It began with six young people, but had since grown to about forty. Those caught in new age cults, drugs, and other vices came, encountered the presence of the Spirit, and gave their lives to Christ. Other such Bible studies had been launched throughout the city as well.

---

4   Genesis 3:24, Numbers 22:23, Joshua 5:13, and 1 Chronicles 21:16 are Scriptural examples of angels appearing with weapons in their hands.

After hearing his story, I told him about our unusual prayer meeting back in the third week of June. I then asked him when they first launched their "Living Room" gathering, and after pausing for a moment, he said it was in the third week of June as well! I believe that our praying in the Spirit in England helped prepare the way for the activity of the Spirit in Amsterdam.

CHAPTER 4

MOST EARNESTLY AND PERSISTENTLY

Sam Cerny

> *For what thanks can we render to God for you, for all the joy with which we rejoice for your sake before our God, night and day praying exceedingly that we may see your face and perfect what is lacking in your faith? Now may our God and Father Himself, and our Lord Jesus Christ, direct our way to you.* (1 Thessalonians 3:9-11)

Torn Away

"*But we, brethren, having been taken away from you for a short time in presence, not in heart, endeavored more eagerly to see your face with great desire.*" (1 Thess. 2:17)

In 1 Thessalonians 2:17, Paul is writing to the church in Thessalonica, and Acts 17:1-10 describes his first visit to that city. While there, he and his team preached for three weeks (17:2-3), and many came to the Lord (17:4). Shortly afterward, some Jews became jealous, formed a mob, and started a riot in the city (17:5-9). The persecution reached a feverish pitch, and late one night Paul and Silas were secretly taken out of Thessalonica and sent off to the city of Berea (17:10).

So Paul and his team were only in Thessalonica for just over three weeks. Usually, when a new church was planted in a city, they stayed for a much longer time to disciple the new believers, but that was not the case in Thessalonica. When Paul says they were *"taken away,"* he uses the term *aporphanizo*, which is a strong term literally meaning to be orphaned or torn away from one's family. It was a sudden and painful separation. Thus we can see why Paul had *"great desire"* or intense longing to see them again. We can understand why it was so urgent that he return to continue teaching, discipling, and fathering them. However, when Paul and his company tried to return to Thessalonica, what happened?

But Satan

"Therefore we wanted to come to you—even I, Paul, time and again—but Satan hindered us." (1 Thess. 2:18)

Before we delve further into this verse, we need to ask ourselves, "Who is Satan? What is the devil?" For to understand this passage, we need to understand who Paul's enemy was. The Bible commences with *"In the beginning God created the heavens and the earth."* (Gen. 1:1) Those heavens were not just the visible sky and universe, but also the invisible realms of glory, and along with the creation of the heavens was the creation of the angelic hosts. This is clarified in Nehemiah 9:6, *"You alone are the LORD; You have made heaven, the heaven of heavens, with all their host, the earth and everything on it, the seas and all that is in them, and You preserve them all. The host of heaven worships You."* Who were these hosts that were created when the heavens were created? They are not visible stars, but rather invisible angelic beings who continually worship the Lord. This same term is also used for angels in 1 Kings 22:19, Psalm 103:20-21, and other verses.

In passages like Ezekiel 1, 10, and Revelation 4, we read that of these created angelic beings, at least four of them are called cherubim and surround God's throne. Moreover, they guarded the garden of Eden, which was God's original tabernacle on earth (Gen. 3:24), and were also represented as carved statues over the ark, which stood in the most holy place of the Tabernacle of Moses (Exod. 25:17-22) and of the temple of Solomon (2 Chron. 5:7-8). Of all the creatures in the universe, the cherubim are in the closest proximity to the Lord's literal, manifest, and enthroned presence. In essence, they function as the chorus leaders of the universe and also play a key governmental role as well.

So how does this pertain to Satan? Various Old Testament prophecies describe this angelic being before and during his original fall into sin such as Isaiah 14:12-15 and Ezekiel 28:11-19. In his depiction, Ezekiel reveals that Satan was originally a cherub. "*You were the anointed cherub who covers; I established you; you were on the holy mountain of God; you walked back and forth in the midst of fiery stones. You were perfect in your ways from the day you were created, till iniquity was found in you.*" (Ezek. 28:14-15)

However, at some point in time, he sinned and became proud, and at that moment he was cast from the Lord's presence. "*So I drove you in disgrace from the mount of God, and I expelled you, guardian cherub, from among the fiery stones. Your heart became proud on account of your beauty, and you corrupted your wisdom because of your splendor. So I threw you to the earth . . .*" (Ezek. 28:16-17 NIV)

Along these lines, Paul reminds us that a leader should not be "*a new convert, lest being puffed up with pride he fall into the same condemnation as the devil.*" (1 Tim. 3:6)

Furthermore, when he was cast down, multitudes of angels followed him. Speaking of Satan and those fallen angels, John said, "*His tail drew a third of the stars of heaven and threw them to the earth.*" (Rev. 12:4) Later on, these stars are identified as angels when we read, "*And the dragon and his angels fought.*" (12:7)

So now that Satan has been cast down, where is he? From where does he advance his evil agenda? Generally, the devil's influence covers the entire planet. Jesus called him the *"ruler of this world"* (John 12:31, 14:30). Paul designated him the *"prince of the power of the air, the spirit who now works in the sons of disobedience."* (Eph. 2:2)

Specifically, though, Satan may choose to concentrate his base of operations from a particular place or person. At times he inhabits specific geographic regions. *"I know your works, and where you dwell, where Satan's throne is . . . even in the days in which Antipas was My faithful martyr, who was killed among you, where Satan dwells."* (Rev. 2:13) At times he resides within specific people. *"And having dipped the bread, He gave it to Judas Iscariot, the son of Simon. Now after the piece of bread, Satan entered him."* (John 13:26-27)

Also, like an army, demons act as generals, lieutenants, soldiers, and other positions under Satan's leadership. Yet where are they? From where do they advance their wicked agendas? Generally, these beings exert their influence around the world from heavenly places.

Paul speaks of *"principalities . . . powers . . . rulers of darkness of this age . . . spiritual hosts of wickedness in the heavenly places."* (Eph. 6:12)

Specifically, demons may choose to concentrate their base of operations from distinct places or people. At times a demon may occupy a specific geographic region. *"But the prince of the kingdom of Persia withstood me twenty-one days; and behold, Michael, one of the chief princes, came to help me, for I had been left alone there with the kings of Persia."* (Dan. 10:13) *"And he answered, saying, 'My name is Legion; for we are many.' Also he begged Him earnestly that He would not send them out of the country."* (Mark 5:9-10) At times a demon may dwell in or upon a specific person. *"Now the Spirit of the Lord had departed from Saul, and an evil spirit from the Lord tormented him."* (1 Sam. 16:14 NIV) *"Now it happened, as we went to prayer, that a certain slave girl possessed with a spirit of divination met us."* (Acts 16:16)

So from these specific geographic locales or individuals, what do the devil and his demons do? What is their ultimate agenda? What is their aim? And what does God allow them to do?

Hindered Us

"Therefore we wanted to come to you—even I, Paul, time and again—but Satan hindered us." (1 Thess. 2:18)

God and Satan are not equals. God is the Creator, and Satan is simply a created being. There is no contest between God and Satan.

In fact, Satan can only go as far as the Lord allows. Consider what Jesus said to Peter, *"Simon, Simon! Indeed, Satan has asked for you, that he may sift you as wheat."* (Luke 22:31) From whom did Satan have to ask permission? The Lord.

Satan knows that he cannot stop God, so he tries to stop or hinder us, God's people. This word *"hindered"* in Greek is *enkopto*, which is a combination of *en*, meaning in or into, and *kopto*, meaning to cut. In essence, this word was "used of 'impeding' persons by breaking up the road or by placing an obstacle sharply in the path."[1] It can be translated as stop, hinder, detain, or impede. This passage says that Satan stopped Paul and his company, but it does not say how he stopped them. We do not know if Satan was using religious persecution from the Jews or political pressure from the Romans or some other means.

When Satan or his demons try to hinder us, how are we to respond? In Paul's case, how did he respond?

Night and Day Praying Exceedingly

"For what thanks can we render to God for you, for all the joy with which we rejoice for your sake before our God, night and day praying exceedingly that we may see your face and

---

1   Vine, William E., *Vine's Expository Dictionary of Old and New Testament Words* (W.E Vine, 1940)

perfect what is lacking in your faith? Now may our God and Father Himself, and our Lord Jesus Christ, direct our way to you." (1 Thess. 3:9-11)

Satan had barred Paul from visiting the church in Thessalonica. Paul was one of the most mature Christians to have ever lived, and if Satan could hinder him, he can stop us. Yet Paul did not accept this hindrance from Satan as inevitable or unalterable. No, Paul and his team fervently responded to this satanic attack, but how?

They prayed *"night and day"* and *"exceedingly"* for the Lord to clear a way for them to go to Thessalonica. Some in the church teach that we only need to say, *"I rebuke you, Satan,"* and that is all that is required. At times that is true. Jesus and the apostles demonstrated that. At other times, though, that is not true. Sometimes Satan and his minions are so entrenched with a certain people, place, agenda, or ideology that continuous, earnest prayer is needed for spiritual breakthrough. This word translated as *"exceedingly"* literally means above and beyond what is expected, superabundant in quantity, or exceedingly excessive.

Sometimes victory over darkness is contingent upon God's people praying night and day, continually, earnestly, and fervently. Part of that earnestness means praying instead of sleeping and fasting instead of eating. Remember that Paul often engaged *"in watchings, in fastings."* (2 Cor. 6:5 KJV)

The Bible is replete with examples of excessive and extravagant responses in prayer and fasting to counteract demonic resistance. Daniel prayed and fasted for twenty-one days (Dan. 10:2-3), and it took exactly twenty-one days for the Lord's angels to push through the hindrance of the demonic ruler of Persia (Dan.10:12-13). Jesus fasted and prayed for forty days before *"the devil left Him, and behold, angels came and ministered to Him."* (Matt. 4:11) The disciples tried to cast out a more powerful, more fortified demon, but were unable. In response, Jesus said to them, *"This kind* [i.e. there are different kinds of demons] *can come out by nothing but prayer and fasting."* (Mark 9:29)

Eventually, Paul's persistent prayer was answered, and Satan's hindrance was removed. God did clear the way for Paul and his team to visit the Thessalonian church, but that did not transpire until approximately five years later during Paul's third missionary journey (Acts 19:21, 20:1-2). For Paul, this was not just a battle fought for weeks or months, but for years.

Clearing the Way

One of my first experiences of persistent prayer and the removal of demonic impediments happened while attending Esperanza High School in Yorba Linda, California, in the late 1980s. Upon entering high school, I was very shy. I desperately wanted to witness openly about Christ, but I could not muster up the courage. At that time, in our youth services at church I heard a constant stream of messages about being a bold witness and taking our schools for Christ. Yet the more messages I heard, the more hopeless, worthless, and guilty I felt. I genuinely wanted to see multitudes of students saved, but I did not know how to overcome my own shortcomings.

"God, what I am going to do? What should I do?" I prayed often. Then the Lord told me to walk around the perimeter of the campus and pray for His kingdom to come. I did this month after month. Then He directed me to walk through the walkways, hallways, and even up and down the aisles in the classrooms praying for His kingdom to break in. So I did this, but very covertly. I would walk throughout the campus praying in English and in tongues very quietly under my breath, and more months passed.

One night I had a dream, and in it I was riding my bike to school, and looking up I saw a dark, foreboding cloud hanging over it. An intense oppression emanated from it. As I rode closer and closer to the school, this cloud seemed to grow heavier and heavier resisting my movements. I began pedaling slower and slower. As I drew near the side gate where I entered the school grounds, I could barely move. Waves of depression started rolling over me. Suddenly, I woke up feeling horrible. I then realized that the lack of witnessing and salvations at my school were not just due to my reticence, but to demonic resistance.

Those days and weeks of praying continued. Then one evening, my parents, some friends, and I were praying in our living room for Esperanza High School. Sitting on our couches and offering requests, it was a normal and somewhat boring prayer meeting. Suddenly, all of us heard with our ears a very loud scream or moan from the hallway, yet there was nobody in that part of the house. Just then an evil presence rushed into our living room. I could actually see a shadowy, grotesque creature standing in the passage way between our living room and hallway. Cold winds also started blowing in the room, and we could all feel them. The temperature actually dropped. We were shocked, slightly scared, and at first did not know what to do. Then we sternly rebuked this demon, lifted up our hands, and started praising the Lord. Eventually, the demon fled, and the sweet presence of the Holy Spirit filled the room. Over and over we sang, "Hallelujah, hallelujah," and then sang in the Spirit.

In those days, God's kingdom truly began to break in. One afternoon a boy named Nick asked if I could give him a ride home from school, and I said yes. I had met Nick before, but hardly knew him. We stepped into my Subaru, and on the dashboard was a large, orange sticker that said, "Smile, God Loves You." Seeing it, he asked, "Are you a Christian? I've been praying and praying to meet another Christian here at the school." He too was a committed Christian. We were both so excited to meet each other.

On the way to his house, we first stopped at my house, and in my living room held a fifteen minute prayer meeting for revival for Esperanza. Over the next few months we pursued the Lord together and encouraged each other to share our faith.

Nick turned into a bold, fiery evangelist. One day I was walking into the Language Arts building, and I saw Nick standing near the wall with Eric, one of the wildest punkers at our school with spiked hair, a leather jacket, chains, and tall laced-up leather boots. Nick's hand was on his shoulder. "What are you doing?" I mouthed to Nick. "We're praying," he mouthed back. Later Nick told me that he was praying with Eric to receive the Lord.

One day in health class, I started talking to a boy next to me who apparently did not know the Lord. He had just been in a car accident, and his neck was severely sore and stiff. Soon the class ended, and students started pouring out of the building. In the middle of that crowd, I told him about how Jesus heals and asked if he would like prayer. He agreed, and so right there I laid my hand on his neck, prayed, and he was healed!

The Lord moved in our midst and touched many people. Eventually, our lunchtime Bible study grew to about thirty students. Early morning prayer meetings in the middle of campus also started. God showed Himself to be faithful, and a couple of years of persistent prayer paid off.

CHAPTER 5

APPEALING TO THE HIGHEST GOVERNMENT

Sam Cerny

Therefore I exhort first of all that supplications, prayers, intercessions, and giving of thanks be made for all men, for kings and all who are in authority, that we may lead a quiet and peaceable life in all godliness and reverence.
(1 Timothy 2:1-2)

The Priority of Prayer

"Therefore I exhort first of all . . ." (1 Tim. 2:1)

Paul begins 1 Timothy 2 with the words, *"Therefore I exhort . . ."* This word *"exhort"* is *parakaleo* meaning "to admonish, exhort, or urge one to pursue some course of conduct."[1] With this word, Paul is showing the urgency of what he is about to say.

Paul continues with writing, *". . . first of all . . ."* This is not first in timing or order, but in importance. With this

---

1   Vine, William E., *Vine's Expository Dictionary of Old and New Testament Words* (W.E Vine, 1940)

phrase, he is showing the priority of what he is about to say.

This introductory phrase reveals that the activity that Paul is about to describe is the one of the most urgent and most important activities that the church can engage in. So what activity is he about to depict? Not teaching, counseling, evangelism, healing, feeding the poor, or a host of other good works. No, what he describes is prayer, and in particular, praying for the government.

The Power of Governmental Intercession

"... *that supplications, prayers, intercessions, and giving of thanks be made far all men, for kings and all who are in authority* ..." (1 Tim. 2:1)

If prayer does not affect the government, then Paul would not urge us to pray for the government. This exhortation only makes sense if this type of intercession is effective. Moreover, prayer affects governmental rulers in two realms—the heavenly and the earthly.

To understand this reality, we need to understand how the apostles and prophets viewed governmental systems over nations. For behind human rulers, angelic and demonic rulers were influencing their decisions either for righteousness or wickedness.

This reality becomes clear as we see the biblical terms describing these rulers, for these terms are used interchangeably between human and angelic beings. Consider these examples: In the book of Daniel, the words *sar* (prince) and *melek* (king) are used for earthly rulers (1:1, 7; 2:2; 9:6, 8; 10:1; 11:5) and heavenly rulers (10:13, 20, 21). In the letters of Paul, the words *huperokay* (authority), *hupereko exousia* (governing authorities), *exousia* (authorities, powers), *arkone* (rulers, princes), and *arkay* (rulers, principalities) are used for earthly rulers (Rom. 13:1-3; 1 Tim. 2:2; Tit. 3:1) and heavenly rulers (Rom. 8:38; Eph. 2:2, 3:10, 6:12; Col. 1:16, 2:15).

Since rulers in the invisible realm are directly influencing rulers in the visible realm, there are aspects of government that cannot be affected simply by petitions, protests, or votes. Some aspects of government can only be affected by prayer.

The Bible is very clear that through our prayers, God moves angels and demons who in turn move presidents, senators, judges, governors, mayors, and other officials. As an Old Testament example, think of Daniel. After seventy years of captivity in Babylon, Daniel offered *"prayer and supplications with fasting"* (Dan. 9:3) for the Jews to return to Jerusalem and rebuild the city as prophesied by Jeremiah. As a result of his prayers, an angel appeared and says, *"At the beginning of your supplications the command went out, and I have come to tell you, for you are greatly beloved."* (9:23) What is the command that went out as a result of Daniel's intercession? The angel continued, *"Know therefore and understand, that from the going forth of the command to restore and build Jerusalem . . ."* (9:25) It was the command from God to release the exiles and send them back to Jerusalem to reconstruct it. As a result of this command, we read that *"the Lord stirred up the spirit of Cyrus king of Persia, so that he made a proclamation throughout all his kingdom."* (Ezra 1:1) That proclamation was a royal decree to release the Jewish captives to return to Jerusalem to restore the city.

So when Daniel prayed and fasted, a command went forth from God's throne room, an angel was dispatched in the heavenly realms, and a king's heart was moved in the earthly realm. Then the law regarding the Jewish captives was instantly changed.

As a New Testament example, consider the church in Acts 12. A time came when *"Herod the king stretched out his hand to harass some from the church."* (Acts 12:1) Thus he had James killed (12:2) and Peter imprisoned (12:3-4). So the early church gave themselves to *"constant prayer"* (12:5) regarding this matter. As a result of their prayers, one angel was sent to the prison to free Peter (12:6-10), and another angel was sent to slay King Herod while sitting upon his throne (12:21-23).

Then, with the political pressures from Herod removed, the gospel spread more quickly and more widely. *"But the word of God grew and multiplied."* (12:24)

So when the early church prayed, angels were dispatched in the heavenly realms, a wicked king was removed in the earthly realm, and the political persecution from Herod against the church at that time was curtailed.

Also, Paul not only tells us to pray for governmental leaders in 1 Timothy 2:1, but he also tells us how to pray for them. He gives us the goals of governmental intercession in 2:2.

The Removing of Disturbances

". . . that we may live a quiet and peaceable life. . ." (1 Tim. 2:2)

As governmental officials are influenced by God through our prayers, we will be better able to live a *"quiet"* and *"peaceable"* life. About these two terms, *"eremos* denotes quiet arising from the absence of outward disturbance; *hesychios* tranquility arising from within."[2] The essence of both words is quietness and peace due to a lack of disturbances. In other words, it is much easier to navigate one's way across the sea in calm weather rather than in a hurricane, for the pelting rain, howling winds, and mountainous waves can make it almost impossible to move forward.

In the context of 1 Timothy 2:1-2, those disturbances are governmental decisions and political realities that can hinder the church's work. Those could include the restricting of movement among towns or cities, the outlawing of public gatherings, the censoring of media, the banning of gospel preaching, the criminalizing of Christian speech, the spreading of false ideologies, and so forth.

Notice that there is a direct connection between praying *"For kings and all those in authority"* (2:2) and living *"a*

---

2 Vincent, Marvin R., *Vincent's Word Studies in the New Testament* (Wordsearch Corp., 2007)

quiet and peaceable life" (2:2) and the desire for *"all men to be saved and to come to a knowledge of the truth"* (2:4). In other words, through our intercession God will move on governmental leaders to help lessen the disturbances and provide a more optimum context for the spreading of the gospel.

The Guarding of Morality and Dignity

". . . in all godliness and reverence. . ." (1 Tim. 2:2)

As government officials are influenced by God through our prayers, we will better be able to live in all *"godliness"* and *"reverence"*. To comprehend this reality, we need to understand the meaning of these two terms.

"Godliness" is *eusebia* which refers to morality as defined by God. Thus, this term refers to how we live. It refers to "a manner of life . . . to conduct relative to self, others, and God."[3] Paul understood that the truth we receive affects how we live. *"Paul, a servant of God and an apostle of Jesus Christ for the faith of God's elect and the knowledge of the truth that leads to godliness (eusebeia)."* (Titus 1:1 NIV) He understood that what we are taught affects how we live. *"Teaching us that denying ungodliness and worldly lusts, we should live soberly, righteously, and godly (eusebos) in the present age."* (Titus 2:12)

The ideologies coming from rulers will help determine the level of godliness in society. The teachings coming from the leaders will help influence the level of morality in the nation. As we pray for our governmental leaders, we need to pray that they would inundated with light, truth, biblical teachings, and prophetic exhortations. Solomon wrote, *"If a ruler listens to lies, all his officials become wicked."* (Prov. 29:12 NIV) So in prayer we need to counteract lies such as the redefining

---

3   Bromiley, Geoffrey W.; Kittel, Gerhard; Friedrich, Gerhard, *Theological Dictionary of the New Testament* – Abridged Edition (William B. Eerdmans Publishing Company, 1985).

of marriage as something other than between a man and a woman.

"*Reverence*" is *semnotes* which refers to dignity as defined by God. This term can be defined as "the characteristic of a thing or person which entitles to reverence and respect, dignity, majesty, sanctity."[4] In other words, everyone is to be treated with the utmost respect, reverence, and dignity because that is the way God treats them.

We are to highly value others because God highly values them. For example, Paul wrote that a bishop should be "*one who rules his own house well, having his children in submission with all reverence (semnotes).*" (1 Tim. 3:4) Children are to respect their parents because God so highly esteems fatherhood and motherhood.

Thus, in regard to the government, their laws should protect the dignity and sanctity of every person regardless of his or her ethnicity, economic status, gender, or age. Great harm comes when that ceases to be the case. In the book of Esther, a specific law was enacted to kill the Jews solely because of their ethnicity. "*If it pleases the king, let a decree be written that they be destroyed.*" (Esther 3:9) In response, Esther and the Jews fasted and prayed for God to change the king's heart and have this decree reversed (4:15-16), and He answered their prayer. God restored their dignity in the eyes of the king, and their lives were saved.

As we pray for our government, we need to pray for leaders and laws that would uphold the dignity of every person. To kings it was written, "*Speak up for those who cannot speak for themselves, for the rights of all who are destitute. Speak up and judge fairly; defend the rights of the poor and needy.*" (Prov. 31:8-9 NIV) So in prayer we need to counteract legislation that dehumanizes and devalues people such as the lawful enslaving of black people, the lawful prostituting of young girls, or the lawful killing of unborn children.

---

4   Thayer, J. H., *Thayer's Greek-English Lexicon* (Wordsearch Corp., 2005)

Releasing Justice

On 7/7/07, I attended The Call Nashville with my brother Tim. The atmosphere in that stadium was electric as about seventy thousand people gathered to worship, intercede, and cry out to God for America. At one point, Lou Engle shared about God's desire to end abortion in America, and then with LIFE tape on our mouths, we silently prayed for the unborn. My heart was deeply touched, and tears fell from my eyes.

The next day I was at the airport in Nashville to board a flight to Las Vegas, where I had to work for a couple of days. Many young people were at the gate with red LIFE bands on their wrists, and so we started talking with each other. One girl said that she had never spoken in tongues before. However, during the time at The Call when we prayed to end abortion, the Spirit fell upon her, and she started speaking in tongues. While hearing her story, again my heart was profoundly stirred.

That evening I landed in Vegas and phoned my wife Brooke, who was in California. The previous day she had tried hour after hour to watch The Call Nashville on god.tv, but the video streaming was down most of the day. Of the twelve-hour broadcast, she was only able to view one hour later in the day when Lou spoke about God's heart to end abortion and then led the crowd in prayer. While watching, the Spirit mightily descended on her, and she broke out weeping and sobbing. She was crying so intensely that our five-year-old daughter Keilah ran into the room saying "What's wrong mommy? What's wrong mommy?" Brooke assured her everything was okay. As I listened to that account over the phone, again my heart started burning regarding this issue.

Over the next few days, Brooke and I sensed that God wanted us to join the prayer movement to help reverse Roe vs Wade and end abortion in America. So we decided to start a Bound4Life chapter where we lived in Orange County, California. However, for this to work, we would need our pastor's approval since we would host prayer rumbles in our church building and recruit members from the church body. We didn't know how favorable he would be, though, to our request. Historically, our church usually stayed away from issues considered political, and they were not connected in any way with The Call, IHOP, Bound4Life, or other similar prayer ministries, either. Furthermore, Brooke and I also made a decision to tell nobody about our plans to start a Bound4Life chapter until we received our pastor's permission. Our plan was to talk to our pastor on Sunday, July 22.

On Friday afternoon, July 20, I taught a workshop at a worship conference our church was hosting that week. My topic was the second coming of Jesus, and my text was Psalm 45. About fifty people attended, and after the workshop everybody left the room except for me, my wife, and my friend Tony who led worship. Then, suddenly, an older lady walked back in the room, approached me, and introduced herself. She did not attend our church, and I had never met her before. She said that the Spirit directed her to come back and tell me something. She then told me that she and her friend stand in front of an abortion clinic every week and pray for the ending of abortion. I was shocked! During the workshop, I had not mentioned anything remotely connected to that. I told her that in two days I was scheduled to meet with my pastor to ask permission to start a Bound4Life chapter in Orange County. I explained how we would lead a prayer rumble at our church once a month and do a LIFE Siege in front of the main Planned Parenthood clinic in the county once a month. That was the very clinic she had prayed in front of for years. She said that she and her friend would be our first members. For me, that encounter with her was an amazing confirmation from the Lord.

That Sunday arrived, and our pastor gladly gave his permission. Then for 2007 and into 2008 we sieged the Planned Parenthood clinic, and we prayed for the doctors and nurses to be saved, for the unborn babies to be rescued, for pro-life messages to be spread throughout the media, and so forth. One of our main prayers was from Ezekiel 4:16, "*He then said to me: 'Son of man, I will cut off the supply of food in Jerusalem.'"* We prayed continually that God would cut off the political, cultural, and financial support to Planned Parenthood. Following that season of sieging, something startling happened in March 2009. The Orange County Board of Supervisors voted to cancel a yearly contract between the county and Planned Parenthood, where almost $300,000 was given to them for sex education in the schools. Regarding the vote to stop the funding, an article in the Orange County Register said, "Planned Parenthood shouldn't receive county funding for its health outreach programs because it also performs abortions, which are morally wrong. That's what county Supervisors said this morning when they unanimously decided to suspend a contract with the nonprofit organization, amid an hours long debate about abortion rights and county contracting policies."[5] Planned Parenthood fought back, and a couple of months of political wrangling ensued after that vote. However, in the end, the funding to Planned Parenthood was not granted.

Moreover, during that time Brooke and I took over a Wednesday night young adult home group. One of the ladies who attended actually worked at Planned Parenthood. As we began to befriend her, she also started bringing her boyfriend who knew the Lord when he was a young child, but had since turned away from Christ and was not walking with Him at all. Eventually, she quit working at Planned Parenthood, he repented and returned to the Lord, and I had the privilege of baptizing both of them in the ocean. They also decided to get married and asked if I would speak at their wedding, which would be held at the chapel in our church. As we talked, she added that all of her co-workers from Planned Parenthood would be attending the wedding as well.

The day arrived, and her co-workers actually closed the clinic down early so that they could come to the wedding.

---

5   http://totalbuzz.ocregister.com/2009/03/10/supes-terminate-planned-parenthood-grant-citingabortions/ 14261

With all of them watching me from the seats, I stood on the stage and essentially shared the whole gospel with Joel 2:13 as my text. However, what we saw in small measure, God wants to do throughout the nations on a much larger scale. He is raising up a massive army of intercessors to resist abortion throughout the earth.

CHAPTER 6

LIVING AN INNOCENT LIFE

Sam Cerny

I want you to be wise in what is good, and simple concerning evil. And the God of peace will crush Satan under our feet shortly.
(Romans 16:19-20)

Having the Right Attitude

"*I want you to be wise in what is good, and simple* [innocent] *concerning evil.*" (Rom. 16:19)

As we look at contending against false ideologies and confronting demonic strongholds, it is critical that we think rightly about Satan and his schemes. If we stand against demonic deceptions and wrestle against demonic beings while carrying the wrong attitudes, we are setting ourselves up for much unnecessary harm. So what is the right attitude in spiritual warfare? What is the proper approach?

We are not to fear Satan or his hosts. We need not cower before demons. The psalmist declared, "*You shall not be afraid of the terror by night . . . nor the pestilence that walks in darkness, nor of the destruction that lays waste an noonday.*" (Psalm 91:5-6) In Luke 10:19 Jesus quotes Psalm

91:13, *"You shall tread upon the lion and the cobra, the young lion and the serpent you shall trample underfoot,"* and in the full context of Luke 10: 17-20, Jesus clearly refers to the serpents and other creatures referenced in Psalm 91:13 as representing demonic spirits, not just natural animals. Additionally, other scholars see other references to demons in Psalm 91 as well. For instance, one professor of theology writes, "Along the same lines, Isaiah 34:14 refers to Lilith, who will inhabit Edom after it is rendered desolate. Lilith was well known throughout Mesopotamia as a demon who was believed to attack people, especially children, at night. This same demon may be referred to in Psalm 91:5, which speaks of the 'terror of the night.' . . . Also on the basis of such parallels, many scholars argue that references to 'the pestilence that stalks', and 'the destruction that wastes at noonday' in Psalm 91:6 are references to demons of pestilence and plagues commonly believed in throughout the Mesopotamian area."[1] Thus in Psalm 91:5-6, the psalmist firmly says not to be afraid of demons!

So why should evil spirits never be feared? Because speaking of our attitude toward demons (1 John 4:3), John wrote, *"You are of God, little children, and have overcome them* [antichrist spirits], *because He who is in you is greater that he who is in the world."* (John 4:4) We need to consider the sheer greatness, power, and authority of the Lord, for when we really comprehend Him, we will fear nothing or nobody but Him. *"Do not fear what they fear, and do not dread it. The Lord Almighty is the one you are to regard as holy, he is the one you are to fear, he is the one you are to dread."* (Isa. 8:12-13 NIV)

We are not to be impressed with Satan or his minions. Though they are supernatural beings that can perform powerful feats, signs, and wonders, we are not to give them

---

1   Boyd, Ph.D., Gregory A., *God at War* (Downers Grove, IL: InterVarsity Press, 1997), p. 82

even an ounce of honor, praise, or glory. All glory is to be the Lord's alone. *"I am the Lord, that is My name; and My glory I will not give to another, nor my praise to graven images."* (Isa. 42:8)

We are not to be arrogant before Satan and his demons. It is one thing to be confident in Christ, but another to be proud in ourselves, our positions, or our reputations. We should not approach any heavenly being with slanderous statements, boastful words, or any type of swagger flowing out of our own pride. James warned of such an attitude when writing about godless men: *"In the very same way, these dreamers pollute their own bodies, reject authority and slander celestial beings. But even the archangel Michael, when he was disputing with the devil about the body of Moses, did not dare to bring a slanderous accusation against him, but said, 'The Lord rebuke you!'"* (Jude 8-9)

We are not to be fascinated by demons or their doctrines. With spiritual darkness and wickedness, there is an element of seduction involved. John wrote, *"These things I have written to you concerning those who try to deceive you."* (1 John 2:26} This word *"deceive"* is *planao*, and it can also mean to seduce or lead astray. In this context, this same word is used in Revelation 2:20, *"Nevertheless I have a few things against you, because you allow that woman Jezebel, who calls herself a prophetess, to teach and seduce (planao) My servants to commit sexual immorality and eat things sacrificed to idols."* It is also translated as *"entices"* in the Greek version of Deuteronomy 13:6, *"If your brother, the son of your mother, your son or your daughter, the wife of your bosom, or your friend who is as your soul, secretly entices (planao) you, saying, 'Let us go and serve other gods . . .'"*

In regards to demonic realms, occult practices, witchcraft, lustful images, or any other such wickedness, fascination is the first step to seduction, and seduction can lead a person into deeper darkness. Some well-meaning intercessors have spent too much time, money, and energy studying and researching the demonic activity in their community or region, and in doing so, they have crossed that line from gaining information to cultivating fascination. This is a dangerous line to cross. We should be fascinated with the beauty of Christ, not the activity of demons.

We are not to tolerate anything in our lives, homes, or church community that would promote or exalt darkness in any way. That could include books, movies, video games, art pieces, or anything else that clearly espouses something wicked, demonic, or idolatrous. It could also mean being careful about what thoughts we entertain or conversations we engage in. Regarding this, Paul exhorted, *"But now you must rid yourself of all such things."* (Col. 3:8 NIV) John also wrote to the church, *"Little children, keep yourselves from idols."* (1 John 5:21)

Our aim is not to be afraid, impressed, arrogant, fascinated, or tolerant, but simply aware of what the enemy is doing. If we want to stop him through the authority of Christ, then we need to know where and how to stop him as the Lord leads. God will be faithful to give us the information we need to pray and obey effectively. This is what Paul encouraged. *"In order that Satan might not outwit us. For we are not unaware of his schemes."* (2 Cor. 2:11) Along these same lines, Peter exhorted, *"Be sober, be vigilant* [alert, watchful], b*ecause your adversary the devil walks about like a roaring lion, seeking whom he may devour."* (1 Pet. 5:8)

The principle underlying these exhortations is in Romans 16:19, *"I want you to be wise in what is good, and simple* [innocent] *concerning evil."* While we should be aware of darkness, let us never become experts in darkness. We need to maintain a real simplicity and innocence in our relation to demonic, evil activity. Moreover, living out Romans 16:19 is not just a good idea or principle, but a necessity for genuine victory in spiritual warfare.

Standing Triumphantly

"And the God of peace will crush Satan under your feet shortly." (Rom. 16:20)

In this verse, Paul is referencing one of the earliest prophecies in Scripture, where God told Satan, *"I will put enmity between you and the woman, and between your offspring and hers; he will crush your head, and you will strike his heel."* (Gen. 3:15 NIV) Eventually, the offspring of Eve would crush the head of the serpent, who is the devil himself. *"That serpent of old, called the Devil or Satan."* (Rev. 12:9) Clearly, Jesus as both fully man and fully God is the ultimate fulfillment of the prophecy in Genesis 3:15. At the cross, while Jesus' heel was bruised, Satan's head was crushed. *"'Now is the judgment of this world; now the ruler of the world will be cast out. And if I am lifted up from the earth, will draw all peoples to Myself.' This He said, signifying by what death He would die."* (John 12:31-33) However, that crushing that already happened in the past is being realized now and will be fully realized in the future.

What Paul says in Romans 16:20 is staggering, though. This crushing is happening and will happen not just under the feet of Christ, but under the feet of the church in Christ. *"Under your feet."* (16:20) We are participants in the fulfillment of Genesis 3:15. We are part of that company that crushes Satan.

Some scholars see in Romans 16:20 only a global, future and final fulfillment at the end of the age. However, others see a more local and partial fulfillment based on the context of Romans 16:17-20. In verses 17-19, Paul warns the Roman church about those who are causing divisions, putting obstacles in their paths, spreading false teachings, and deceiving Christians, and then in verse 20, Paul attributes that activity not just to divisive people, but to Satan himself. Thus, he saw that darkness being resisted and crushed under the feet of the church in Rome. Both interpretations of Romans 16:20 are likely correct.

However, verse 20 begins with the word *"and,"* which clearly links it to verse 19. This is paramount to understand. Our ability to be wise in what is good and innocent concerning evil will directly affect our ability to crush the schemes of Satan in our midst. If we fail to do the former, we will not be able to do the latter.

God's Prescription

Upon our arrival in Lhasa, Tibet, in September 1993, our team became the first foreign students ever to study at Tibet University. Our courses included studying Tibetan language, culture and Buddhism. At one point, I eagerly wanted to understand Tibetan Buddhism, so my Tibetan friends took me on many tours of various temples and monasteries. In those idol rooms, devotees would prostrate, chant, beat cymbals, give offerings, and light butter lamps, and the light of those flickering flames would reflect off of the idols scattered throughout. I could literally feel the suffocating presence of spiritual darkness in those places. At the same time, I found myself studying the idols and wall murals depicting scenes from Buddhist mythology, somewhat arrogantly rebuking the demons, and being fascinated by the mystery of it all. Then something unexpected started happening.

During worship at a Wednesday night prayer meeting, my mind became filled with terrifying visions of Buddhist protector deities, which are portrayed in all kinds of violent and gruesome ways in the back idol rooms of monasteries. Though I tried, I could not rid my mind of those images.

Following that night, accusations and condemnation increasingly filled my mind as well. It seemed like every sin I ever committed was recalled. Moreover, night after night I experienced horrific nightmares and attacks from evil spirits. Late one night as I slept, I dreamt that the door of my dormitory room opened, and a animal-like creature walked in and sat on the chair of my desk. It just stared at me. I woke up frozen in fear.

One night, I felt so overwhelmed by my own sinfulness, that I did not even feel like a Christian anymore. After crying out to God for help, I grabbed my Bible and randomly opened it, and my eyes fell on Psalm 103:10, *"He has not dealt with us according to our sins, nor punished us according to our iniquities."* Those words filled my heart with such joy and thankfulness! God had truly spoken to me, and the truth of that verse brought such lightness and freedom to my soul.

However, when I woke up the next morning, the same oppression continued on. One afternoon I was sitting on my bed trying to pray, but my words seemed to bounce off the ceiling above. It seemed that God had left me, and I despaired. I no longer had any sense of His presence at all.

I didn't share my troubles with anyone else, because being the youngest member of our team, I was afraid they would think I couldn't handle the difficulties and pressures of Tibet. Finally, though, during another Wednesday night prayer meeting, I could take it no longer. After the meeting finished, I told my leader what I had been experiencing and asked him to pray for me. He laid his hand on me and immediately rebuked some evil spirits by name. Just then it seemed like a dark, heavy cloud lifted off of me, and I sighed and bent forward with my face to the carpet. The power of the Spirit shot through me like a bolt of electricity.

With my face bent down, I immediately became aware of a mighty angel standing right before me, and feeling the fear of the Lord, I was too overwhelmed to look up. Then these words hit my heart like the blast of a trumpet: "I want you to be wise in what is good, and simple concerning evil." That was God's prescription for my folly. After that, I experienced such glorious freedom, and that oppressive darkness did not return. That was a lesson I never forgot, and Romans 16:19 is a verse I've tried to live by ever since.

CHAPTER 7

ANATOMY OF A CONTENDING HOUSE: PART 1

Lou Engle

> *And I also say to you that you are Peter, and on this rock I will build My church and the gates of Hades shall not prevail against it. And I will give you the keys of the kingdom of heaven, and whatever you bind on earth will be bound in heaven, and whatever you loose on earth will be loosed in heaven.* (Matthew 16:18-19)

Live up to Your Name

These words of Jesus and the mind-bending implications of them shatter all earthly boundaries as to the measure of authority, power and influence Jesus has given to his praying church. Not even the gates of Hades, the powers of death, of which nothing on earth is stronger, shall exceed the church in strength. It is a statement, which if laid hold of by faith, could redefine our expectancies for breakthrough in every place and circumstance where Satan boasts of his dominion.

If this is true, and these are the "red-letter edition" words of Jesus, then every gate of hell and every spiritual power can be potentially overcome and prevailed against by the church. If this is true, then it becomes the obligation and the marching orders of the church to become the church that Jesus declares it to be. The story is told of the great general Napoleon walking through and examining his troops. He came to a young man who stood shaking and trembling before the mighty military leader. When Napoleon asked the young man's name, the soldier responded fearfully, "My name is Napoleon." The general said, "Young man, live up to your name or change it." It is time for the church to live up to its name, which is this essential, defining purpose that Christ gave in Matthew 16:18-19.

Jesus called us by the name *"church"*, which in Greek is *ecclesia*. The *ecclesia* was a ruling body of a Greek city-state (for an example of this term used in that context, see Acts 19:39). It would be like the city council over your town or city. Jesus transfers the meaning of that ruling body to his church. Here He is clearly giving us His glorious intentions for what the church that He builds would be.

It was not just to be a gathering of believers coming together for worship and sharing a common life. It was to be a ruling body called out by God to exercise spiritual authority and dominion over every spiritual and earthly institution of oppression and over every control center of injustice. It was to be a war council of the highest measure, exercising through prayers and decrees the weapons of binding and loosing which thrust heaven into earth and bar hell's invasion of this planet.

The words *"gates of Hades"* refer to the powers of death which Paul describes in Ephesians 6:12 as principalities and powers, rulers of darkness of this age, and spiritual hosts of wickedness in heavenly places. Gates were the places where the ruling body of a city would meet. This is where governmental transactions took place and war councils were held. The gates of a city defended that city and were immoveable. Therefore, when Jesus says, *"The gates of Hades shall not prevail,"* He is declaring that the church is attacking the gates of demonic control centers and satanic war councils. These are not the gates of hell attacking the church, but this is the church attacking these gates through the offensive prayer weapons of binding and loosing.

In Matthew 18:18-20 Jesus again declares, *"Assuredly I say to you, whatever you bind on earth will be bound in heaven, and whatever you loose on earth will be loosed in heaven. Again I say to you that if two of you agree on earth concerning anything that they ask, it will be done for them by My Father in heaven. For where two or three are gathered together in My name I am there in the midst of them."* Here Jesus gives further definition to the exercise of binding and loosing, for He places it in the primary context of a unified company agreeing together in prayer.

So, as we call forth a movement of contending prayer, which is a primary job description of the *ecclesia* that Jesus builds, let us examine the anatomy of a contending house of prayer. The following are some essential elements that we believe God has given to us in our experience of establishing Justice Houses of Prayer in several cities across America and in launching a movement of prayer strike teams that are taking prevailing prayer into regions where there is great spiritual opposition and strategic ideological strongholds.

The constitution of the community is more important than the passion of its worship or the fervency of its prayers.

When Jesus said, *"If two of you agree on earth concerning anything that they ask"* (Matt. 18:19), He is describing much more than a mental assent to a prayer focus. He is describing the constitution, nature, unity and the purity of a covenantal band brought together by the Spirit and through praying in the Spirit. The whole context of the binding and loosing in Matthew 18:21-22 deals with this constitution of the church, the *ecclesia*, this praying, ruling company. Jesus' command that we forgive our brother *"seventy times seven"* (Matt. 18:22) means that we are always to forgive completely and continuously. Then in 18:15-17 Jesus says, *"Moreover if your brother sins against you, go and tell him his fault between you and him alone. If he hears you, you have gained your brother. But if he will not hear, take with you one or two more, that 'by the mouth of two or three witnesses every word may be established.' And if he refuses to hear them, tell it to the church. But if he refuses even to hear the church, let him be to you like a heathen and a tax collector."*

These two passages sandwich the Scripture concerning binding and loosing and agreeing in prayer. Here Jesus is saying that if the church is going to exercise spiritual authority in prayer, its relationships among each other must be right, there must be no unconfessed sin, and no brother or sister persisting in a rebellious and stubborn unwillingness to turn from known sin can be allowed to continue running with that community.

Psalm 24:3-4 says, *"Who may ascend the hill of the Lord (the place of spiritual authority)? . . . He who has clean hands and a pure heart."* The hill of the Lord is the place of His governmental authority. To exercise authority over the gates one must be walking in an experiential position of holiness. You cannot rule over darkness if darkness is ruling your company. You cannot bind the spirit of pornography if the spirit of pornography binds you. Now, we are not talking about perfection here. God knows our weaknesses, failings and besetting sins. A person struggling with sin who is broken over it and yearning to change is not excluded from the ruling body. But it is the secret, unconfessed sin that a person refuses to turn from that can shut down the effective agreement of prayer and hinder the ability of the *ecclesia* to bind and rule over the powers of darkness in a specific region.

The expanding house of the prayer movement that Jesus is building is not simply a new form or different method of church where people can escape discipline and the spiritual government of leaders. It is not just a place where we can come so that we can play our instruments and enjoy the presence of the Lord. You can have a house of prayer where different worship teams are taking shifts, and members of those teams may be filled with secret sin. A house of prayer that contends for spiritual authority over powers of darkness cannot afford such compromise.

In Acts 19, we see seven sons of Sceva who sought to exorcise evil spirits in the name of Jesus whom Paul preached. The demon answered them saying, *"'Jesus I know, and Paul I know; but who are you?' Then the man in whom the evil spirit was leaped on them, overpowered them, and prevailed against them, so that they fled out of that house naked and wounded."* (Acts 19:15-16} Notice the word *"prevailed."* Prevailing will not be accomplished with assumed authority. The church prevails with real authority based on the constitution of its community. This is why in every one of our houses of prayer or strike teams, we take communion regularly and call the young men and women to confess their sins one to another and reconcile relationships so that the blood of Jesus could cover our praying band.

Again, the constitution of the community must be agreement. In the early days, where God was establishing the spiritual DNA of the Justice House of Prayer, a dream was given to us where the Lord gave us the words "Covenant will open the door." For every prayer assignment when God has brought together a community of prayer, we publicly commit in a covenantal way, which is really Christianity 101, not to speak against any person in the praying band. We commit to confess our sins one to another and to work out relationships where there is wounding and breakdown. Because we live our house of prayer experience in a community context, difficulties always arise. But, we understand that this public transaction and commitment to unity is a very foundational basis for victory against the gates of hell. "*A house divided against itself will not stand.*" (Matt.12:26) Jesus gave this word in the context of casting out demons, binding the strongman and loosing the captives (12:26-29).

In the natural, the Marines have this level of camaraderie and commitment. Their covenantal watchword is Semper Fidelis meaning "always faithful." They will not leave a wounded soldier on the battlefield. They are committed to rescue the one who is down. Their survival depends on moving together under united command. This is why in our houses of prayer there are no conscientious objectors. When we go to war, we go together. We must show grace where there is weakness, but where there is rebellion, discipline in love must take place.

A casual approach to the prophetic assignment can bring casualties, not just to the praying company, but to those whom we are seeking to liberate from the strongman's chains. When Elisha commanded the king to strike the arrows and he only struck three times, the prophet Elisha was angry and said, *"You should have struck five or six times; then you would have struck Syria till you had destroyed it! But now you will strike Syria only three times."* (2 Kings 13:19) How many innocent lives were taken by the Assyrian armies because of a passive response to the prophetic assignment? This brings us to the next key element of a contending house of prayer.

There must be a clear moral objective.

When Jesus said, *"the gates of hell will not prevail,"* he spoke generally, but when the Macedonian man appeared to Paul in a night vision saying, *"Come over to Macedonia and help us"* (Acts 16:9), the focus and moral objective of Paul's assignment become very clear. Several years ago, I was on a prayer assignment with Dutch Sheets and others in New England. We had gone to Harvard during the day to pray, but did not achieve a sense of breakthrough in our intercession. Dutch talked to me that evening saying he felt that we had not completed our assignment. I was in agreement with my friend, and we decided to do a night strike. As we left, we didn't know exactly how to get to Harvard and actually became lost. We knew, though, that we were in the general vicinity because so many students were walking around in the restaurants and local stores.

Finally, we saw a dimly lit street and determined that we would go, park, and pray there.

At that spot was a gate entrance to a lawn that was surrounded by faintly lit buildings. Each of us walked in different directions and began to pray. Suddenly, Dutch called me to come and join him. There we stood in front of the philosophy building of Harvard and engraved across that building we could see the words, "What is man that Thou art mindful of him?"

Dutch was amazed as he told me that this was the very building that he had written about in one of his books. The story was this: Years ago the president of Harvard asked the head of the philosophy department what he wanted engraved on the front of the new philosophy building that was being built. The philosophy department-head wanted the words "Man is the measure of all things" to be inscribed there. So construction began, the scaffolding went up, and a canvas was draped over the area. When the canvas was pulled down, the president had overruled the philosophy department-head by engraving the words, "What is man that Thou art mindful of him?"

What are the chances that wandering in the dark of night, driving around lost, and hoping that we were somewhere on the Harvard premises we would drive into a dark street and walk right into the very place that Dutch had written about? This was no coincidence.

This was a prophetic flashpoint. We knew this was the staging ground of a great battle against the spiritual powers of humanism dominating Harvard and the modern day educational systems of America. It was in this place that I knew we were to build a contending house of prayer. Here we determined to hurl David's stone of "What is man that Thou art mindful of him" at the forehead of the Goliath of humanism's mantra "Man is the measure of all things."

In 2006, after some one hundred young people prayed night and day for forty days near Harvard, we launched the Boston Justice House of Prayer, a contending house of prayer that has not ceased to stand before this building and declare that the spiritual power of humanism will fall before the outstretched rod of God's Word. The reports that we are now hearing of the rumblings of revival and the casting out of demons are now thrilling our hearts. Giants were meant to fall.

Without the prophetic command, "Take that hill!" our prayers are ineffective because there can be no specific agreement. A contending house of prayer must have a clear moral objective. In 1996, a dream was given to me that I would lead thousands of young people up the stairs of the Supreme Court building to do battle against the false ideologies being promoted there. That dream was the first in an amazing series of directed prophetic words that led seventy young people to Washington D.C. to contend against abortion in front of the Supreme Court building. As a result, pro-life judges were raised up and partial birth abortion was ended. A major factor of that victory was that we were not just shooting shotgun sprays of prayer ammunition. We had a clear moral objective and a clear target to hit.

The contending house of prayer must be committed to victory at all costs.

A new attitude must come to the praying church. We do not pray for a feel good experience, but we pray to win. For not to win is to allow Satan to continue to reap havoc on innocent and broken lives. This very moment I am reminded of the movie *Taken* where a father's daughter is taken captive and forced into human trafficking. Suddenly, this father, a retired special ops expert, knows that sex trafficking has a face. The retired becomes re-fired and goes into attack mode warring like a wild-man against a real enemy and rescues his daughter from her wicked captors. Victory was not just optional for this man, for the victim was his daughter. The church needs to recover the agonizing reality that real people are going to a real hell. Drugs, sexual immorality, abortion and sex trafficking are destroying lives. Injustice has a face. When we see that face, prayer will take on a new dimension. It must be victory at all costs.

I believe accumulated prayer that is offered up day by day and year by year will eventually free the captive. However, I also believe that only having a long-term mentality can hinder us from the urgency and travail of breakthrough prayer right now. We must know the moment when God is pressing for victory. I had lost the heart of one of my sons when he was in his early teens. He was in rebellion, yet yearned for his father, and I for him. I got desperate. I fasted 31 days on water praying for my son's heart to be turned back to me. On the 31st day he told me that Jesus was giving him dreams of revival. His heart turned, and the rebellion was broken.

The old saints used to pray until they had a breakthrough. It was called "praying through." Companies of prayer must rediscover this "praying through" mentality where principalities and powers can no longer stand and must give way to the urgency of earth's relentless demand for heaven's answer.

Reese Howells, in the days of World War II, had a company of intercessors that God had forged together into a mighty fighting unit. They were a contending house of prayer. They bore the responsibility of winning real earthly battles through spiritual contention in prayer. Listen to Howells' language from the book: *Reese Howells Intercessor* as he exhorts his company: "You are more responsible for this victory today than those men on the battlefield. You must be dead to everything else but this fight. Because you have committed yourselves you are responsible . . . We are here until these Nazis are put out . . . I am not willing that thousands of our boys should be lost, because there has to be the 'doom of the Nazis' and it will come now if we prevail . . . I want to fight this enemy this weekend as if it were the end of civilization . . . Don't allow those young men at the Front to do more than you do here."[1]

---

1   Grubb, Norman, *Rees Howells: Intercessor* (Fort Washington, PA:

Listen again to the commitment of this band: "Was there anywhere else in the whole of Britain, or America, or elsewhere among God's people another such company, maybe a hundred strong, who were on their knees day by day, holding fast the victory by faith, while soldiers across the water were retreating mile by mile, whole countries surrendering and an enemy in sight of their goal? From this time on through all the years of the war, this company was in prayer every evening from 7 o'clock to midnight, with only a brief interval for supper. They never missed a day . . . There were many special periods when every day was given up wholly to prayer and fasting."[2] Reese Howells actually believed that his praying people were more significant than the soldiers on the ground, and that real wars could be won through prayer.

I am continually stirred by the passage in Exodus 17:8-16 where Moses, Aaron and Hur held up the rod of God on top of a hill while Joshua fought in mortal combat with the Amalekites on the ground. As long as Moses held up his hands, Joshua was winning. But when he would let his hands down, Joshua's army would be pushed back. People were dying or living according to what was being done in the heavenly realm. What a picture of prevailing prayer and the need to recover the life and death desperation and determination that we must gain victory at all costs.

The contending house of prayer is by nature committed to the command of offensive action and attack mode.

In a time of discouragement some years ago, when it seemed that we were losing in the spiritual war all around us, God gave me an encouraging and defining dream. In the dream I was a goalie on a soccer team. The field was slanted toward my goal, and my defense was like a sieve. Our opponent pounded

---

Christian Literature Crusade, 1952
2   Ibid., pp. 249-250

shot after shot at me. Halfway through we were losing 0-5. I then walked into the half time meeting, and my team sat there passive and unconcerned. I said to myself, "I'm done, I'm quitting, I'm outta here!" Then, suddenly, it was like a spirit of prophecy erupted inside of me, and I began to roar, "I'm not a goalie, I'm a striker!" I woke up out of the dream knowing that the Spirit of God was stirring me and calling me to my purpose. The movement of prayer that we were establishing would never be given over to defensive action alone. The answer to seeming defeat was to strike, strike, and strike again.

Jesus, when speaking about casting out evil spirits, described the attack nature of his own personal mission on earth. He said in Luke 11:21-22, "*When a strong man, fully armed, guards his own palace, his goods are in peace. But when a stronger than he comes upon him* (some translations say 'attack him') *and overcomes him, he takes from him all his armor in which he trusted, and divides his spoils.*" Jesus was the stronger one who came to the earth to attack and overpower the strongman, who is Satan himself, and to take the spoil of human souls from his grip. Again, Jesus' purpose in life was that he had come, "*To destroy the works of the devil.*" (1 John 3:8) Our prayer attitude must be to enter a territory, attack, and destroy the works of the devil.

Our fight is not against people. We love people, but we need to reclaim a fighting spirit and rally our souls out of the slumber of peaceful coexistence with demonic powers that are ravaging our friends and families and robbing us of our future.

CHAPTER 8

ANATOMY OF A CONTENDING HOUSE: PART 2

Lou Engle

And shall God not avenge His own elect who cry out day and night to Him, though He bears long with them? I tell you that He will avenge them speedily. (Luke 18:7-8)

A contending house of prayer must be determined to siege the gate of hell until the victory is won.

When we position a contending house of prayer at the gate of an injustice or where a people are in great spiritual crisis or darkness, we are laying siege to a demonic spiritual fortress. To lay siege is to abandon the right to quit. A siege by definition is long-term offensive strategy to compel an enemy to surrender. When a siege is lifted, there can be no victory, for the enemy is then prematurely loosed from the vice grip of God. When we placed our Bound4LIFE siege works at the door of the Supreme Court, we determined not to leave that spiritual stand until abortion ended or the government removed us. The following quote became our siege battle cry, "When the victors when they come, when the forts of folly fall, find my body near the wall." I don't want to be one who just simply enjoys the spoil of war. I want to be a part of a company who sacrificed everything to prevail against the gates and stood until the powers were compelled to surrender.

It is not enough to have major prayer gatherings that push back the powers of darkness. We must then raise up a long-term stand to sustain what we gained in the initial offensive. In a dream the Lord spoke to us strongly, "Wherever The Call goes, I will establish My house of prayer." We have sought to be obedient to that mandate.

Jesus gave us a spiritual principle when he said, "*When an unclean spirit goes out of a man, he goes through dry places, seeking rest, and finds none. Then he says, 'I will return to my house from which I came.' And when he comes, he finds it empty, swept, and put in order. Then he goes and takes with him seven other spirits more wicked than himself, and they enter and dwell there; and the last state of that man is worse than the first. So shall it also be with this wicked generation.*" (Matt. 12:43-45)

Demonic spirits thrive in a vacuum. And when the church does not fill a spiritually vacated place after a breakthrough occurs, those same spirits come back and fill the vacuum, and the situation is worse than before. I will never forget when we prayed at The Call Pasadena that the pornographic industry in Northridge, California, would be shut down. Some time later an AIDS scare swept the whole industry, and the pornographic machine was virtually shut down. The newspapers shouted it. As I read that account, I was struck that this could be God answering our prayers, but then it struck me again that it was now necessary to raise up a contending house of prayer or a citywide altar of continuous worship to fill the vacuum.

I never moved on that inward stirring and to this day as the pornographic industry thrives more than ever, I wonder about the implications of my inaction. How many men's and women's lives could have been saved from the pornographic plague if I had seized the day and sieged the stronghold? We need generals of intercession to rise and direct the prayer forces not just for momentary breakthroughs, but also for long-term restraining of the powers.

A contending house of prayer must gain air supremacy over principalities and powers through extended fasting and prayer.

In July 2004, we gathered fifty young people from across the nation to Colorado Springs, Colorado. God had given us a very clear prayer assignment to pray for the ending of abortion and the raising up of a pro-life president who would appoint pro-life judges. At the beginning of those fifty days, I taught them about Daniel's 21-day fast as described in Daniel 10.

His fasting and prayer inaugurated a war in heaven between holy archangels and the demonic prince of Persia. This dark prince of Persia, an invisible spirit being, is found in this passage playing the puppet strings over the earthly kings of Persia influencing them to promote negative policies directed toward the Jews. Daniel, being deeply concerned about the affairs of his people Israel, set himself to pray and fast for understanding concerning the situation.

After 21 days of spiritual battle, the holy archangel of heaven, with the help of Michael, the angelic prince over Israel, dislodged the demonic prince of Persia from its position of spiritual influence over the kings of Persia and then gained that same place of influence and spiritual supremacy in its stead. The archangel then came to Daniel with a message from heaven: *"Do not fear, Daniel, for from the first day that you set your heart to understand, and to humble yourself before your God, your words were heard, and I have come because of your words. But the prince of the kingdom of Persia withstood me twenty-one days; and behold, Michael, one of the chief princes, came to help me, for I had been left alone there with the kings of Persia."* (Dan. 10:12-13) Some key commentators say that the words, *"For I had been left alone there with the kings of Persia,"* should be better translated "and I remained [as victorious on a field of battle] over the kings of Persia." Daniel's fasting, in cooperation with angelic movement, shifted a whole empire and its policy toward the Jews.

After teaching on Daniel 10, I exhorted those young people with the declaration, "You are the RAF—the Royal Air Force. Winston Churchill said of the RAF, 'Never has so much been owed by so many to so few.' You must win the spiritual battle over the elections through fasting and prayer like Daniel won his victory. You will know if you won the spiritual battle in the heavens during this time of intensive prayer if a pro-life president is elected, and you will know if you lost if a pro-choice president is elected. It is your responsibility along with all the saints who are praying in America to prevail in prayer over this election for the sake of the thousands of unborn children that this election will affect."

The RAF was the Royal Air Force of Great Britain. When Hitler had swept across Europe with his Blitzkrieg lightning-fast military machine crushing every foe and finally compelling France to surrender, the main barrier to a complete European takeover was the island of Great Britain. Hitler set his sights on the military subjugation of this great people.

To take this island, it was necessary for the German air force, the Luftwaffe, to gain air supremacy and destroy the Royal Air Force. With the destruction of the RAF complete, nothing could restrain the war machine of Germany from sweeping Great Britain.

It was in this defining moment of history that the Royal Air Force, outnumbered and outgunned, hurled itself against the superior forces of the Luftwaffe. Day after day and week after week, with hundreds of its courageous pilots being killed, the RAF continued to withstand the great air assault. The German forces could not gain air superiority and finally withdrew from its military objective of the destruction of England.

Prime Minister Winston Churchill was so moved by the RAF's outrageous and sacrificial stand that he uttered to General Ismay, "Don't speak to me. I have never been so moved." After about five minutes he leaned forward and said, "Never, in the field of human conflict has so much been owed by so many to so few." Before this great battle Churchill had declared, "The battle of Britain is about to begin. Members of the Royal Air Force, the fate of generations lies in your hands." I had essentially said the same things to these young people, "The future of America is in your hands. You must gain air supremacy in these elections."

On the 47th evening of continuous day and night worship and prayer, I met David Manuel for the first time, the coauthor of a trilogy of brilliant books on the providential history of America. I told him nothing about my RAF prophecy and asked him to speak that night to those young people. At the end of his message, he suddenly kicked in to what I knew was the prophetic word. He said to those young intercessors, "You are the RAF! Never has so much been owed by so many to so few!" You could feel and almost hear the gasp of amazement that reverberated across that room. Those young people new that heaven had heard and history was being made. A pro-life president was elected, two pro-life judges were appointed, and partial birth abortion is no more.

God has given me a life mandate: to raise up a generation who will give themselves to extended fasting and prayer for breakthroughs against the spiritual forces of wickedness in the heavenly places. The last days generation, as even described in Revelation 12, will so command air supremacy that Satan will lose his position in heaven and be cast down to the earth because he will not be strong enough to resist any longer. Once again the voice of Jesus will be heard in every place where darkness and injustice boasts of its dominion, "I saw Satan fall like lightning."

A contending house of prayer will be marked by day and night intercession in seasons where God calls for breakthrough.

There are certain spiritual strongholds that will not fall, but by day and night prayer. Luke 18 begins with Jesus speaking a parable that, *"Men always ought to pray and not lose heart."* (18:1) He describes the incessant cries of a widow to an unjust judge that demanded justice from her adversary, and He likens that to the prayers of the elect who cry out to God day and night for justice.

Jesus says, *"I tell you that he will avenge them speedily. Nevertheless, when the Son of Man comes, will He really find faith on the earth?"* (18:8) There are certain injustices that will not be moved except by faith in a God who answers sustained day and night prayer.

During the early presidency of George W. Bush, the Senate continually filibustered his pro-life judicial nominees. Through a profound dream, God gave the Justice House of Prayer in Washington, D.C., a prayer assignment. We needed to break the filibuster. The Holy Spirit led us to stand day and night for seventy-two hours in the front of the Supreme Court facing the Capitol building commanding the filibuster to be broken. In the natural a filibuster is literally day and night speech that restrains a Senate vote. It was as if we could see the spiritual powers of darkness "filibustering" God's plans for righteous judges. It was war over the Capitol, and the continuous, outstretched rod of 24/7 prayer could alone break it.

When the next nomination from George W. Bush came up, once again a filibuster was attempted, but this time it had no strong support in the Senate. Satan, we believe, had fallen like lightning and the decree of God for a pro-life justice was delivered. 24/7 prevailing prayer, we believe, won a spiritual battle that brought forth justice for late-term unborn babies.

A contending house of prayer overcomes the powers of darkness through divine intelligence and the spirit of revelation.

A spiritual entrance by divine revelation is needed to bring down every demonic stronghold. By wisdom a king makes war. Paul said we are not ignorant of the schemes of the devil.

After our fifty days and fifty nights of prayer against abortion, a phenomenal series of events took place.

I write in Che Ahn's book, *Reformer's Pledge*, that a young Korean spiritual son of mine maintained a Daniel fast praying for the ending of abortion and for a pro-life president. For two years, he ate no meat or sweets. The day after pro-life President George W. Bush was elected in 2004, the young man said to the Lord, "Unless you confirm to me today that you want me to continue on my Daniel fast I am going to break it at midnight and eat cake." That evening as he walked to his school library to study, he met a young man and introduced himself saying, "Hello, my name is Brian Kim." The student replied, "Hello, my name is Daniel Fast." People are shocked when they hear the story and they laugh, but it's no laughing matter. God was saying, "Young man, you are highly esteemed in heaven. You are moving angels and demons. Go on fasting until this murderous slave trade is expelled from the nation."

There is a new breed of praying, passionate young men and women on the horizon who have been fasting and praying for justice. They may become the *ecclesia* that Jesus spoke about, a people that the gates of hell or the *"powers of death"* could not prevail against (Matthew 16:18). This young man dreamed of a strategy of prayer to target abortion. Fasting opens up revelation. In the dream, people had tape over their mouths with the word LIFE written on it. For five years now in response to that dream, through a ministry called Bound4LIFE people have stood with LIFE tape over their mouths pleading the blood of Jesus over the bloodshed of America crying for mercy and justice. Who would have guessed that the media would have fallen in love with the image and blasted it out on TV news programs, national newspapers and magazines all over the world?

Now, across America thousands have prayed in front of courts and abortion clinics with LIFE tape pleading a 22-word prayer, "Jesus, I plead your blood over my sins and the sins of my nation. God, end abortion and send revival to America." Some 250 Bound4LIFE chapters are now laying siege to the citadel of abortion, and amazing statistics now say that public opinion, even among young people in America, has shifted toward pro-life. One dream from God has created a revolution.

We wrote a poem about the dream nature that describes the counter-cultural bands who pray the dream revelation of God. "If you hang around the Dream King, you get into a dream stream, you join yourself to a dream-team, and you do the Martin Luther King thing." God wants to give his praying companies revelation, and He can do it through the Scriptures, dreams and visions, or through a still small voice. We must not treat the prophetic like a toy. The prophetic can be smart bomb, a spiritual atomic weapon, by which strongholds can be destroyed. In our contending houses of prayer we worship the God who gives secrets in dreams to His people.

Jesus said to His disciples, *"No longer do I call you servants, for a servant does not know what his master is doing; but I have called you friends, for all things that I heard from My Father I have made known to you."* (John 15:15) Many of God's thoughts and secrets are given through the gifts of the Holy Spirit. But He gives them to those who will do something with them, to those who obey His voice.

Our contending houses of prayer hold regular "dream-stream" meetings. We worship, get into the Word, and then let the company share their dreams or what God has spoken to them. Sometimes in these gatherings we feel like we are standing in the very council room of God listening to His strategies and wisdom, and confirmations are given beyond what human beings could make up. Many of these dreams have fueled the prayer movements of The Call, Justice Houses of Prayer, and Bound4LIFE. God's people, like Daniel of old, through revelation and the interpretation of dreams have become the hinge of history. They are God's CIA, Christian Intelligence Agency. Oh, for a people of divine understanding.

ANATOMY OF A CONTENDING HOUSE: PART 2

A contending house of prayer does not just ask God for answers, but they proclaim prophetic, authoritative declarations in prayer.

In 2003, two Call gatherings took place in Los Angeles and San Francisco, and seventy thousand people came to those two solemn assemblies. Between them potentially thousands of Californians fasted for forty days. Prior to The Call San Francisco, I was mobilizing in Sacramento, the Capitol of California. At that time a young man, whom I had never met, came to me. He told me that he had heard me speak on dreams, and so he prayed that God would give him dreams. The Lord answered his prayer by giving him a remarkable dream encounter.

In the dream he was in a stadium prayer event filled with people. There was a platform in that stadium where kings would decree the word of the Lord. He told me that I walked onto that platform and began to make proclamations. The then governor of California was seated in that stadium gathering, and he had to submit to every word that was being proclaimed though he did not want to. The dream ended. I was quite gripped by the potential implications of the dream.

The governor at that time had been passing several laws supporting anti-family legislation. Moreover, His administration was in deep financial trouble. We had a sense that God was going to shake his throne, and we prayed with the word of faith in our hearts for that shaking to happen. Soon after The Call San Francisco, an impeachment procedure was enacted and the governor was removed from office outside of a normal election cycle. In the media it was actually called "the recall." Many would say that this was a natural outcome of the political and financial situation in the state. But could it be that through two solemn assemblies, 40-day fasting, and authoritative prayer a principality over that administration was bound, and the result was the removal of that leader. Daniel said, *"He changes the times and the seasons; He removes kings and raises up kings."* (2:21)

Psalm 110:1-2 gives us a biblical foundation for what that dream and its result may have accomplished: *"The Lord said to my Lord, 'Sit at My right hand, till I make Your enemies Your footstool.' The Lord shall send the rod of Your strength out of Zion. Rule in the midst of Your enemies."* Jesus is seen here sitting as priest and king seated at the right hand of His Father. As priest He intercedes and as king He rules.

Priestly intercession precedes and is foundational to kingly rule and authoritative decrees. Derek Prince, author of *Shaping History Through Prayer and Fasting*, says of this scene, "The rod (the mark of a ruler's authority) is not stretched forth by Christ's own hand, but it sent 'out of Zion.' All through Scripture, Zion denotes the place of assembly of God's people . . . by right of our heavenly citizenship we take our place in this assembly that is gathered in Zion . . . In the world, the forces of evil are rampant on every hand, rejecting the authority of Christ and opposing the work of His kingdom. But, 'in the midst,' the Christians assemble in divine order as kings and priests. Out of their assembly, the rod of Christ's authority, exercised in His name, is sent forth through their prayers. In every direction that the rod is extended, the forces of evil are compelled to yield, and Christ in turn is exalted and His Kingdom advanced."[1]

We look forward to the day when Christ returns, takes up His earthly throne, and brings every enemy underneath His feet. But until that day, we as a contending house of prayer, with the gift of faith, must decree the word of the Lord in the midst of Christ's enemies now. We must continue to remember, though, that our enemies are not people, but spiritual forces of darkness in heavenly places. When God gives us a word of faith in our prayer gatherings, we should cease asking and begin proclaiming, and the Lord's enemies will fall back on every side.

---

1   Prince, Derek, *Shaping History through Prayer and Fasting* (New Kensington, PA: Whitaker House, 1973), pp. 44-45

ANATOMY OF A CONTENDING HOUSE: PART 2

The contending house of prayer must put feet to their prayers.

Jesus said to His disciples, "*'The harvest truly is plentiful, but the laborers are few. Therefore pray the Lord of the harvest to send out laborers into His harvest' . . . These twelve Jesus sent out and commanded them, saying . . . 'Go, preach, saying, "the kingdom of heaven is at hand." Heal the sick, cleanse the lepers, raise the dead, cast out demons. Freely you have received, freely give.'"*(Matt. 9:37-38, 10:5, 7-8)

Prayer, far from being an escape from action, is actually the forerunner and impetus for action, service, and being sent out. Prayer is the force and the foundation of all effective ministry. The church has been big on doing and little on praying. Could it be that our lack of fruitfulness and effectiveness is because we have put the cart before the horse?

When Jesus left the earth, He only left one thing behind: a house of prayer. But that house of prayer released such a supernatural sending out of laborers that the whole known world was turned upside down. I will never forget the night our company, who had been praying for two years for the ending of abortion, was suddenly apprehended by the vision and call of adopting babies as the answer to our prayers. From that point on we have been in an adoption whirlwind. The Call has sought to mobilize adoptions of newborns and children in the foster care system. Furthermore, a foundation for the funding of adoptions was started and an adoption agency established.

When Jesus moves His people to pray, their hearts are broken, and then they are sent as the very answer to their prayers. This is the heavenly pattern. The contending house of prayer must lead the parade of history in acts of justice and compassion. In fact, it is the praying church that God uses to create whirlwind movements of justice and mission that change the world.

The great civil rights movement of the 1950s and 1960s could really be said to have sprung from the African American prayer movement where millions cried to God for freedom and liberty from oppression. God heard and sent forth voices like Martin Luther King, Jr.

Jesus said that His house would be a house of prayer for all nations. Across the world there is a rising movement of prayer like has never been seen. Consider the stadiums filled with solemn assemblies, the prayer furnaces burning in universities across the country, the ten years of day and night prayer in Kansas City and other places of the earth, and the extended fasting and prayer spreading everywhere. And now God is emphasizing the raising up of contending prayer in every sphere of influence and over every mountain of authority.

Years ago we received a dream in which the "L" flew out of the famous Hollywood sign which sits on a hill overlooking the city, and it flew over to Mount Wilson which also towers above the Los Angeles basin. The words then became HOLYWOOD and WILLSON, the will of the Son. The next day after I heard the dream, I received a call from a prayer mobilizer who was in Washington D.C. He started telling me about the prayer mobilization what was soon to take place in Hollywood, and then in the middle of our conversation, he said, "And my son told me this morning that God wants to take the L out of Hollywood and make in Holy Wood." With that confirmation, I knew this was a word from the Lord.

With that promise, for seven years we contended in prayer for Hollywood. At the end of that time, I was scheduled to preach at a church in that city and was planning on sharing the dream. Just before stepping up to speak, a person approached me with an entertainment magazine in his hand, and the main article was entitled "Holy Wood" and was about the release of Mel Gibson's movie *The Passion of the Christ*, which was unbelievably popular and became one of the highest grossing films of all time. When looking at the article, I sensed the Lord whispering to me, "Mel Gibson is the answer to your prayers." Furthermore, I was told that during a television interview, Gibson said that this movie had been on his heart for seven years. God wants a contending house of prayer in Hollywood to pray His will. He wants that city to be holy.

Principalities and powers are being challenged, rulers and judges are being shaken, and souls are being ripped out of Satan's talons.

We have written this book that those who read may run. You are being summoned into a prayer revolution that will shake the thrones of iniquity and prepare the way for the ultimate throne, the eternal reign of Christ.

OTHER BOOKS BY THE AUTHORS

A Moment to Confront by Lou Engle and Sam Cerny
Digging the Wells of Revival by Lou Engle and Tommy Tenney
Elijah's Revolution: Power, Passion and Commitment to Radical Change by Jim W. Goll, Lou Engle and Che H. Ahn
Fast Forward: A Call to Millennial Prayer Revolution by Lou Engle and Catherine Paine
Nazirite DNA by Lou Engle
Pray! Ekballo! by Lou Engle
The Call of the Elijah Revolution by James W. Goll and Lou Engle
The Call Revolution by Lou Engle and Che Ahn
The Jesus Fast: The Call to Awaken the Nations by Lou Engle, Dean Briggs, Bill Johnson and Daniel Kolenda

Made in United States
Troutdale, OR
09/20/2024